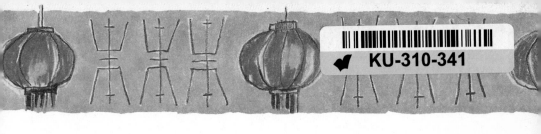

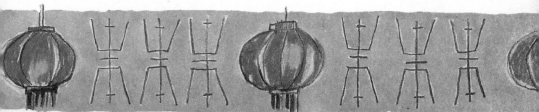

Classic
CHINESE
C·U·I·S·I·N·E

Edited by Rosemary Moon

TIGER BOOKS INTERNATIONAL
LONDON

ILLUSTRATIONS BY
CAMILLA SOPWITH AND ROD FERRING

CLB 4364
This edition published 1995 by
Tiger Books International PLC, Twickenham
© 1995 CLB Publishing, Godalming, Surrey
Typeset by SX Composing, Rayleigh, Essex
All rights reserved
Printed and bound in South Africa
ISBN 1-85501-617-6

CONTENTS

INTRODUCTION

China is an enormous place! It is the world's third largest country, with an area of almost 9.6 million square kilometres or 3.7 million square miles, smaller only than Russia and Canada. It includes more than 3,400 off-shore islands, the largest of which, Hainan, in the South China Sea, is roughly the same size as Sardinia.

The Largest Population

China has the largest population in the world with more than one fifth of the total global population living within its borders. In such an enormous country is not at all surprising that geographical differences have given rise to strong regional identities and traditions, and that these are apparent even today in many aspects of daily life, including China's great cuisine.

Home of the World's Oldest Civilisation

With a recorded history of 3,500 years, China is certainly one of the oldest, if not *the* oldest, of the world's civilisations. Zhonghua, the Chinese name for the country, literally means "central land", reflecting the ancient Chinese belief that the country was the centre of the world and the only true civilisation.

Ancient Chinese skills and technology matched those of the Romans, especially in their ability to make paper and to produce porcelain. These superior skills led the ancient people of China to cut themselves off from the rest of the world, regarding all others as barbarians. This really had little detrimental effect on the country until the Industrial Revolution, by which time China had started to fall behind other developed countries.

It was not until the Communists came to power in China in 1949 that programmes for economic development and social change were introduced that have helped to transform China into a modern nation. Since the 1970s China has sought to return to the international community from its self-imposed isolation, and there is now far greater freedom for the exchange of information and for travel to and from this great country.

The Regions of China

China is divided into many regions for local government purposes but for the explanation of Chinese cuisine four main areas illustrate the differing culinary tastes and traditions. These are the South, based around Canton; the North, where the cuisine includes many great banquet dishes as the Imperial Court of China at Beijing (Peking) was situated here; the East region and the West, which includes Szechuan province, home of much of China's hottest and spiciest food.

The geographical and economic differences between these areas contribute much to the basic differences between the foods. However, many dishes are common throughout China and it is the special foods that were traditionally cooked for banquets and celebrations that really underline the regional differences.

A Great Cuisine in the Tradition of France

The only other cuisine that I have studied that has the same

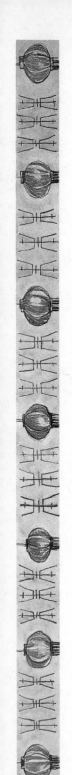

passion for cooking is that of France. France also has a wide variety of climates which are illustrated in its regional cookery. Any book that is to concentrate on French country cooking must divide, or at least research, the recipes by region. Should this also be the case for Chinese cookery? Well perhaps, but I have not done so, as I feel that those who are just beginning to enjoy Chineese cookery will want to look up recipes by the main ingredient and not by the area from which they come.

The purists in classical Chinese cookery, those who take their recipes from the vast selection that have been cooked and used in China for centuries, are skilled in the ancient ingredients and seasonings that make this a truly great cuisine. However, for those of us who are enthusiastic amateurs and newcomers to Chinese cookery, some of the dishes that we know best and which have led us to a thirst for greater knowledge of this cuisine are in fact virtually unknown in China!

The Chinese Cooking of the West

In the nineteenth century many families emigrated from China to Europe and America. Some set up restaurants, sharing their culinary skills and knowledge with a public hungry for their 'new' style of cookery. As time went on and Chinese restaurants became more and more popular, it was easy for customers to assume that the food they were served in the restaurants was indeed the classic cuisine of China. However, as is often the case, one has to adapt to survive and the restaurateurs introduced some dishes to their menus that would appeal to the western palate, had a Chinese flavour but were not strictly classical Chinese recipes. Perhaps the most famous of these is chop suey, one of the most popular of all dishes on the restaurant menu outside China, and yet relatively unknown inside the country, except by those who have had to leave their native shores to discover it! The ubiquitous serving of canned lychees and ice cream for dessert is another such culinary 'invention', and yet it must be popular to remain on so many menus.

The Best of Both Worlds

So, for this collection of classic Chinese recipes I have included some from the truly classical cookery of regional China, as well as some of the most popular dishes found in restaurants around the world. These may not strictly be classics, but they are popular standards through which many of us gain our initial enthusiasm for Chinese food and they deserve a place in both our affections and this book.

Southern China – a Land of Haute Cuisine

We are probably more familiar with Cantonese or Southern Chinese cookery in the west than with any other regional style of Chinese cuisine. This is because the early émigrés who opened the first Chinese restaurants in the west were from this area. Cantonese cooking is widely regarded as the best in China, the haute cuisine amongst an eclectic culinary tradition which still manages to retain local characteristics. Much of the luxurious nature of celebratory Cantonese cooking is attributed to the chefs of the Imperial Court who fled south for refuge from Beijing when the Ming dynasty was overthrown in the seventeenth century. These were the chefs who had the time to experiment with snack foods, or dim sum, that are now such an established part of Chinese cuisine and enormously popular in the west.

Delicacy or Travesty?

One aspect of Cantonese cookery that is much frowned upon in the west is the tradition of experimenting with so-called delicacies or exotic foods. Regretfully these include (or certainly have done in the past) such things as dog and turtle. In most countries the use of popular pets, dogs and cats, as food is very much frowned upon in normal times. Turtles are now regarded as a species to be protected, hence more mock turtle soup is now sold than real. Turtles were on this earth before the dinosaurs and have survived much – we really ought to be making efforts to keep them in existence rather than be killing them unnecessarily for food.

Light Flavours and Seasonings

The cuisine of Southern China explores the natural flavours of foods without heavy seasoning from garlic, chillies and spices although oyster sauce, which is made along the coast, is widely used here as it is throughout China. All Chinese cookery is comparatively quick but the Southern Chinese prefer their food

slightly undercooked, even by Chinese standards. Thus foods retain their colour and texture, making both stir-frying and steaming popular methods of cookery. When cooking in the Cantonese way all your ingredients must be as fresh as possible and in prime condition.

The coastline of this region of China is over 1,000 miles long and provides a rich harvest of crabs, lobsters, oysters and other seafood, the shellfish being as highly prized in China as they are in northern Europe. The main difference in the preparation is that the Chinese are used to cooking their shellfish themselves, ensuring that it is as fresh as possible. Very few people in the west would go to this trouble, although it is now possible to buy raw prawns in most large supermarkets and their flavour is definitely superior to those cooked prior to freezing.

The Rice Bowl of China

Southern China is one of the major rice-growing areas, earning the region the colloquial name of the rice bowl of China. This term is also applied to the Western region, another rice growing area. The cooking of rice is an art, and one of great importance in a cuisine where it is such a staple part of the diet. Rice is used for both savoury and sweet dishes, although the former are far more popular in China.

Rice is also ground into flour and used for noodles, which are popular throughout China. It is also the basic Chinese breakfast in the form of congee, a porridge-like concoction of soft, watery rice.

Northern China – Home of the Imperial Court

The cookery of northern China is perhaps the next most elaborate after that of the south. Vastly different in climate from the area around Canton, the north includes the ancient capital of China, Beijing. It is too cold in the north to cultivate rice and so the staple foods are grains, including wheat and millet. These are often ground into flour and then made into pancakes and dumplings.

Peking Duck – a True Classic?

Well, I would have to say that the answer to that question is no. A modern-day classic perhaps, but not an ancient recipe, handed down through countless generations. However, it is probably the most famous of all Chinese dishes and a great favourite around the world. It is always served with a spicy plum sauce, shredded cucumber and spring onions and pancakes but never with rice. Perhaps it has achieved such popularity outside China because it is eaten wrapped in pancakes? This, however, is a regional means to an end and not a culinary garnish – Peking Duck could not be served with rice which is seldon eaten in the north, whereas pancakes are a staple food.

Another reason why Peking Duck cannot be considered to be an ancient classic dish of China is that very few homes or indeed restaurants, have ovens and the duck for this recipe is always roasted. More of this later!

Three Great Influences

The cooking of northern China, and especially of the area around Beijing, has developed under three influences: the Chinese Moslems, the cooking of the Imperial Place and the peasant cookery of the area.

When Genghis Khan captured Beijing in the thirteenth century he brought with him many of the traditions of the western provinces of China where large animals, such as cattle, deer, pigs and sheep were common and spit-roasting was widely used to cook the meat. Some people feel that this was an early influence on the creation of Peking Duck, and well it might have been.

It is argued that the Imperial Place influenced the cooking of this region less than the Moslems and the local peasant cookery because the last Emperors of China were from Manchuria, an area which has few, if any, specific dishes to call its own. The Manchu or Ch'ing Dynasty actually lasted from 1644 to 1912 and saw the times of greatest stability in China as well as a dramatic decline in the economy and total mismanagement of resources. However, it also saw a marked increase of interest in the Imperial Household in food and, after Emperor Ch'ien-lung visited Canton, tasting the cuisine of the south of his great country, steps were taken to introduce recipes from the south to the north, especially into the Imperial Household, and these eventually influenced the whole cuisine of the region.

The country or peasant cooking of the area contributes the

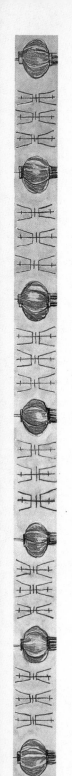

noodle and dumpling or "steamed bun" recipes to the cuisine of northern China. In the harsher and more extreme climate ways had to be found to preserve vegetables for use throughout the winter and dried mushrooms, pickled fruits and vegetables, and smoked and dried meats are all common in this area. Fresh vegetables which store well, like turnips and onions, are also widely used, as are garlic, spring onions and leeks. Confucius was from the northern region of China and probably had a few wise thoughts on the cuisine of the area!

The Land-Locked West

The western region is not only without any sea coast, it is also virtually cut off from the rest of China by mountains. The area includes the Szechuan and Hunan regions and Szechuan cookery is becoming very popular in the west, with its hot, spicy flavours derived from chillies, pickles and other seasonings. Szechuan peppercorns, much used in this area, are hot and distinctive and should be sought out for Chinese cookery.

Szechuan is situated in the fertile valley of the upper reaches of the Yangtze River which, at 5,520 km (3,430 miles) long, is the longest river in Asia and the fifth longest in the world. The Yangtze actually has the largest, most populated and the most fertile valley of all the great rivers and has been renowned for its fertility for at least 2,000 years. Hunan is similar to Szechuan in that it too is situated in a river basin, that of the Han, a tributary of the Yangtze. Both regions enjoy the same climate, one of hot, sultry summers and relatively mild winters. People of the world's hotter climates often enjoy a hot and spicy diet and the western Chinese follow suit, using copious amounts of garlic, onions and ginger in conjunction with red chillies.

A Feudal Flavour

In this fertile and productive area of China there has always been a flourishing agriculture and plentiful fruits and vegetables. Pork is popular as are poultry and fish, although the region relies on rivers for fish as it has no sea coast. The vast areas of land to be worked have necessitated a feudal approach to life in this part of China with workers or peasants and landlords, both of whom were ruled by warlords. The cookery of the area very much reflects these social differences with the majority of food being plainer, usually steamed, and yet still fiery in flavour, using all the local seasonings. The warlords and some of the landlords enjoyed a more elaborate style of eating, combining more flavours into each dish and usually toning down the robustness of the hot pepper seasonings. These upmarket dishes were slightly more akin to the cooking of the north but retained the regional ingredients and flavours of the western provinces.

Fu-Yung, a Favourite in Szechuan

Fu-yung, a popular dish based originally just on egg whites and not the whole egg, is perhaps a surprisingly mild dish to be a favourite in this region of highly spiced foods, but popular it is. Many people now refer to any dish that includes eggs as a fuyung, whereas in terms of classical Chinese cookery it should indicate only the whites of eggs, mixed with cornflour and minced chicken and then fried. Stock might be added to the fried chicken to make a sauce to serve with vegetables or other rather bland dishes to give more flavour. Any vegetable can be prepared in this way, making cauliflower, carrot, cabbage or whatever fu-yung, but the secret of preparing the dish well is to poach or steam the vegetables until soft before quickly stir-frying them with the fu-yung to finish the dish without overcooking and toughening the eggs.

The Eastern Region

Last but not by any means least amongst the culinary regions of China is the eastern region. This area stretches inland to central China from the east coast and includes the largest city and busiest port in the country, Shanghai. The lower valley of the River Yangtze provides a wonderfully fertile river plain and this area, where many fresh fruits and vegetables are grown, is particularly noted for its vegetarian dishes. The Yangtze and the coastline ensure plentiful supplies of fish throughout the region; indeed, there seems to be plenty of everything here.

A Land of Plenty

The great abundance of food allows for all sorts of culinary experimentation and there are many excellent restaurants of international repute in and around Shanghai. Vegetarianism is more popular amongst those who are better off and can afford to pick and choose their food. In the eastern region, where all foods are plentiful, there is sufficient choice to make an interesting meatless diet.

The Best Ingredients and the Lightest of Sauces

With so many ingredients available in absolutely first class condition, eastern cooking tends to be light, and the sauces and seasonings added to food are mild so as not to mask the natural flavours of the prime quality ingredients. Steaming is a very popular method of cooking and great lengths are taken to accentuate the flavour of the principal ingredient of each dish. Soy sauce, the most popular of all Chinese seasonings, is produced here; indeed the best soy sauce in all China is produced in the eastern region as is the best vinegar, Chingkiang, used both as a seasoning and a dipping sauce.

Sugar, adding Sweetness and Richness

Sugar grows well in the eastern region and the people of this area are said to have a sweet tooth! They certainly use sugar in many of their recipes, and add it to savoury dishes to accentuate flavours – it is often used with fish, meat, shellfish and vegetables. There can be no doubt that a little sugar in a western beef casserole at the end of the cooking adds richness and a roundness of flavour – well, the same applies here and, when combined with the use of oil, sugar has earned the area a reputation for rich and lavish food.

Vegetable and Fried Rices

The eastern region certainly grows a good crop of rice, the area's staple food. In many other regions rice is almost always boiled or steamed but in the east there has been much experimentation leading to numerous dishes of fried vegetable rice. This might just include one vegetable, stir-fried to release its flavour, and then added to the rice during boiling or steaming. The vegetable, be it onion, leek or something more exotic, then flavours the rice during the cooking process.

Fried rices have become especially popular with western enthusiasts for Chinese cookery. Perhaps this is because boiled rice can become a little dull and relies so much upon the food that it accompanies. In China fried rice is a snack, a complete meal in itself, which explains why there are often so many ingredients in what is otherwise a staple food. It would never be served in a traditional meal setting, being too flavoursome and complex to accompany other dishes. When eaten in restaurants outside China, fried rice requires only one dish to accompany it to provide a satisfying meal.

Eating in the Chinese Way

Eating Chinese food in the traditional way is a very different experience to formal or informal meals in almost any other

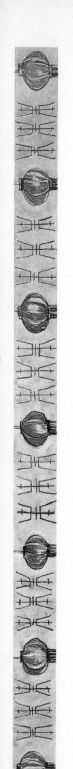

culture. The majority of us are conditioned to eating a starter or soup, followed by a main course and a dessert, with some cheese, either before or after the pudding, if the meal is to be a little more lavish.

Chinese meals are not served in this way, except at grand parties and formal banquets. For everyday eating and home entertaining a selection of dishes are prepared for the meal, but they are all laid out as a spread and served pretty much simultaneously, with soups (usually one or two) served more as drinks than as starters. Dim sum, either sweet or savoury snacks, might be included in the meal, almost as punctuation marks, to refresh the palate at various stages, but this is more common at parties or banquets. Wine is seldom served and neither, surprisingly, is tea, except at banquets; the Chinese rely on their soups as drinks, which is why most varieties are little more than flavoured or garnished stocks.

A typical family meal would usually consist of one or two soups and four or five main dishes, all chosen to provide contrast in colour and texture and a variety of fish, meat and poultry. Most Chinese main courses include some vegetables but a separate vegetable dish might also be served, along with the staple of the area, be it rice, wheat or millet, pancakes or dumplings.

Puddings – a Special Treat

Puddings or desserts are seldom served except on special occasions, at parties or at banquets. There are comparatively few classic dessert dishes and the best known of the limited selection is Eight Jewel or Eight Treasure Rice (see page 243), a lavish moulded pudding revered in the same way as the western Christmas Pudding. What few desserts the Chinese do have don't really measure up to the western idea of a pud. and in most cases, both in China and abroad, the best way to finish a Chinese meal is with a lusciously ripe piece of fresh fruit.

The Chinese do, however, have a tradition of sweet dim sum, little mouthfuls of delicious petit-four-like creations, which are served in tea houses. These are popular with Chinese and Westerners alike, and dim sum, both sweet and savoury, are often served in cafés in Hong Kong where it is not uncommon to find people making a complete meal out of ten or twelve different varieties of these snacks.

Banquets and Big Occasions

Chinese people never have to look very far to find an excuse for a party. Food on these occasions is of prime importance and is served in a slightly different way to a family meal. Indeed, a banquet is served in a style much more akin to a western meal.

Guests at a banquet might expect a selection of cold dishes to be served on arrival, in a similar manner to anti-pasti at the start of an Italian meal. The next selection of dishes are usually hot, dry fried foods, almost like warm cocktail savouries. Wine will be served throughout a banquet.

The meal then progresses with a vast selection of dishes being presented to guests in small groups, allowing them time to savour each 'course' as it is presented hot and freshly cooked. Many meats and a selection of fish dishes will be included and perhaps as many as four or five different concoctions of rice. In the north, where grains and dumplings are more common than rice, the heavier foods such as dumplings will be reserved for the end of the meal, so that guests might enjoy a wide variety of dishes without getting too full too early on!

Desserts will be served with a selection of the wonderful fruits grown in China, both fresh and preserved.

Well, I feel full just having written about that! Suffice it to say that it was common to serve around 60 dishes at a banquet and at the grandest of all occasions, the All-China Manchu Banquet, around 300 were served! Such lavish entertaining is now less common, despite the fact that the Chinese are still passionate and most particular about their food, enjoying every opportunity that presents itself to show hospitality and to share good fortune. Things are being scaled down gradually to more sensibly-sized celebrations, with less wastage and extravagance.

The Ancient Centre of Vegetarianism

Vegetarianism is not new, it has been practised for many hundreds of years by certain sects of the Bhuddist faith and much of the tradition of a meatless diet stems from the Bhuddist monasteries of China. I first came across lo-han vegetables at our local Chinese restaurant and they are delicious – the lo-hans are minor gods of the Bhuddist faith. Vegetables cooked in this style are served in a light but savoury gravy and have a

delightfully fresh fragrance. Single vegetables or a mixture of two or three, or vegetables mixed with tofu or bean curd for extra protein, are all delicious when prepared in the style of the lo-hans.

A Very Healthy Diet

Very few Chinese, even today, have ovens which means that the vast majority of Chinese dishes are cooked over an open fire or on a hob. The cooking methods are simple and the most popular are steaming and stir-frying. Most dishes are cooked quickly in just one pot or wok and are simple to assemble – no wonder woks are so popular today amongst the students of the west!

Stir-frying is such a healthy way to cook. Only the minimum amount of oil is required and the food is cooked quickly, retaining many of its vitamins and minerals. It is very interesting to compare the following average daily intake of calories in the west with a typical Chinese diet:

	W. Europe	N. America	China
Daily intake	3,050 calories	3,170 calories	2,060 calories
Protein	11.3%	11.9%	11.6%
Fat	35.8%	41.5%	13.7%
Carbohydrate	52.9%	46.6%	74.7%

It simply cannot be healthy for Europeans to eat over two and a half times as much fat as the Chinese and for Americans to eat over three times as much.

Special Ingredients for a Special Cuisine

There are many ingredients which are essential to good Chinese cooking and which were virtually unheard of in the average western household until just a few years ago. I suppose that we have known about soy sauce since Chinese restaurants first became popular, but did we know that there are light and dark varieties?

Some of the more unusual ingredients are still hard to find unless you have a Chinese supermarket close by, but these are becoming more common in major towns and cities so check your commercial telephone directory. Large supermarkets also stock a fair selection of canned vegetables and fresh herbs suitable for Chinese and Oriental cookery, as well as basic stir-fry sauces. However, as 'Chinese-flavoured' food enjoys increasing popularity, more and more varieties of sauces and ingredients are being produced with exotic sounding names but which are not strictly correct for Chinese cookery, or which are recommended for an incorrect use. For example, I recently bought some fine rice noodles which were recommended for adding to stir-fries but which would have been much better used for adding substance to a soup, which is how the Chinese would use them.

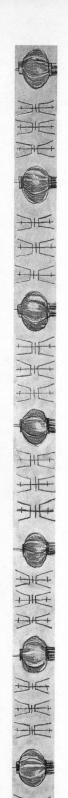

What Is It?

To help you through the maze of exotic ingredients called for in some of the following recipes here is a brief run-down of what is what:

Soy Sauce A basic seasoning sauce which has a salty flavour and is used instead of salt in most Chinese cookery. It is made from a mixture of soya beans, flour and water which is naturally fermented and then matured. The best soy sauce comes from the area around Shanghai. Of the two types of soy sauce light soy is the saltier and is best for general cooking, whereas the dark is matured for longer and is more suitable for rich meat dishes and stews.

Black Beans Chinese black beans are not to be confused with the small black kidney beans of South America. They are soya beans fermented with salt and spices and are usually sold canned outside China. Rinse the beans in cold water before use. Any leftover beans can be stored in a sealed container in the refrigerator for many weeks.

Chinese Mushrooms Many varieties of mushrooms are used in Chinese cookery, both fresh and dried. Outside China most of the mushrooms are dried – they look rather strange but do have a wonderful flavour. It may not be possible to obtain all the varieties called for in the following recipes unless you have a specialist Chinese supermarket or grocer nearby. The mushrooms will keep for ages so look out for them when you have the opportunity. Straw mushrooms are only available in cans and should be rinsed in cold water before being used.

Szechuan Preserved or Pickled Vegetables This is a pickled vegetable root, preserved in salt and hot chillies. It is hot and crunchy and is an unusual and pungent addition to many Szechuan dishes. The pickle should be rinsed and chopped before use. If it is not available, I would suggest using a hot Indian-style pickle –

it will not be the same and purists will throw up their hands in horror, but it will introduce some fire to your cooking.

Spring Roll & Wonton Skins Both of these papers, skins or wrappers are very thin and rather difficult to make at home. Make life a little easier for yourself and buy fresh or frozen wrappers from a Chinese grocer.

Sugar Chinese sugar is processed differently from that available in the west. For most accurate results use granulated sugar or the pale brown coffee crystal sugar.

Rice Wine This is rich and mellow and is made from glutinous rice and spring water, fermented with a little yeast. A good quality pale dry sherry is the closest alternative but the Chinese would consider it to be a poor substitute for rice wine.

Oils Groundnut or peanut oil is the best to use for Chinese cookery, although corn and vegetable oils also work well. The very fragrant sesame oil is seldom used for cooking by the Chinese but is added as an extra seasoning at the last moment to prepared dishes.

Bean Curd, Doufu, or Tofu Tofu is actually the Japanese name for bean curd but it is the name by which it is mostly widely known in the west. It is a solidified paste made from ground yellow soya beans. There are two varieties available in most supermarkets, a solid variety for stir-fries and most general cookery, and a smoother silken tofu which is softer and therefore more suitable for soups. Silken tofu is generally a long-life product and may be found on the supermarket shelves, whereas the fresh blocks of solid tofu will be found in the refrigerated cabinets. Tofu is more of a texture than a taste but is widely used in Chinese cookery and is valued in vegetarian cookery the world over as a very rich source of vegetable protein.

These are the basics of the Chinese larder. Other ingredients are discussed in individual recipes and, as interest in all types of

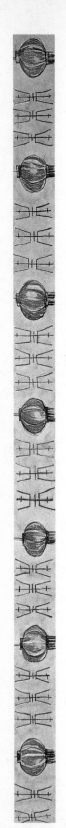

cookery continues to grow, it will become increasingly easy to obtain the ingredients with which to make authentic Chinese food.

The Versatile Wok

All you need now before you can start cooking in the Chinese way is a wok! Of course you can use a frying pan, but a wok is designed in such a way that only a small surface area is actually in contact with the heat, so that once food is cooked it can be drawn up the sides of the wok to keep warm whilst preventing overcooking, leaving the hottest area ready for the next ingredient to be added. This cannot be done in a frying pan so exactly the same results cannot be achieved as in a wok.

Woks need not be expensive, indeed the best ones are often made from relatively thin gauge metal that conducts heat easily and rapidly. Electric woks and cast-iron woks have been introduced in the west, but neither would receive rave reviews in China! Buy a wok with a lid and a trivet so that it can also be used as a steamer. Seasoned well with oil when new, according to the instructions supplied with it, your wok should last for years.

The Art of Using Chopsticks

Well, I'll just give you a little tip – keep the bottom stick firmly clasped and move the top one; well, that's how it works for me! Good luck!

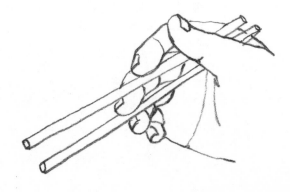

SOUPS

Soup formed the major part of many diets for centuries, when cooking techniques were limited and the available equipment was often just one pot over an open fire. In many of the great cuisines of the world it is almost possible to trace the development of a race through their soups, seeing how prosperity and an ever increasing range of both cooking equipment and ingredients led to soups becoming less substantial, a less important part of the meal, then eventually becoming light and of infinite variety, to be served hot or cold, and usually as a starter.

Very little in China changed for thousands of years. Life in the country simply carried on and traditions in the home remained virtually unchanged, so it is reasonable to assume that many of the soups that are eaten in China today have been popular for many, many years.

Soup as a Drink

It is quite usual to have two or more varieties of soup within the course of a typical Chinese meal. Soup is not eaten as a first course, a starter to whet your appetite, but as a part of a running buffet-style of meal. Many Chinese regard a bowl of soup as we would a glass of wine, to be dipped into when the palate is dry whilst feasting on other meat, fish or poultry dishes. This is why the vast majority of Chinese soups are what we would call "thin" or clear soups, often little more than a well-flavoured stock with a vegetable or pasta garnish. These thin soups are easier to drink down. Wine, water or even tea are not traditionally served in China to accompany a family meal.

Thick Soups for Special Occasions

Anyone used to dining in Chinese restaurants in the west might reasonably assume that Crab & Sweetcorn, Chicken & Sweetcorn and any other of the numerous soups thickened with this starchy vegetable are truly classic Chinese dishes. Well, they may be old Chinese recipes but they are not considered to be such classics as the many varieties of clear soups. However, there are some highly prized thicker soups which are often served as part of a banquet or celebratory meal, when the soup is served in the western style, before the main meat, fish and poultry dishes.

Of all the thick soups the most special treat for the Chinese gourmet is Shark's Fin Soup. Shark's fin is a great delicacy and, even in China, it is expensive. The fin itself has comparatively little flavour – what it adds to the soup is the texture that makes this dish so special. The fin is sold dried and has to be soaked, preferably overnight, before use.

Good Stock – Good Soup

The secret of a good Chinese soup is exactly the same as that of any other soup from any other country in the world – a good stock! As many of the thin soups are little more than stock with garnish it is easy to see that a depth of flavour is vital if the soup is to be enjoyed.

As so many Chinese dishes require meat, poultry or game there is never any shortage of bones and trimmings for making stock. Do not throw the carcass away after preparing a dish of duck – boil it up with a few fresh vegetables to make a rich and versatile stock. However, care should be taken when making game stock as it can become a little 'gluey' or musty in flavour – this is easily rectified by adding some chicken bones to the stockpot.

Never cover the pan when making stock – this affects the flavour and can also make the stock cloudy, which would be disastrous for a Chinese clear soup. Add plenty of herbs and peppercorns for flavouring but do not season the stock with salt until it has been strained and reduced, otherwise the resulting liquor may be over flavoured.

Stock freezes very well. After preparing a pan of stock reserve some for immediate use – it will keep for about five days in the refrigerator if it has been prepared from a fresh carcass. Boil the remaining stock until well reduced and freeze in small, usable quantities and preferably in blocks – it then takes up less room in the freezer. Add extra water, wine or sherry to the defrosted stock before using.

PEKING SLICED LAMB WITH CUCUMBER SOUP

Most Chinese soups are 'thin' or clear soups, based on a good homemade stock. This soup is a little more substantial than most as it includes very finely sliced lamb fillet. Boneless leg of lamb could also be used.

Serves 4-6

Ingredients
225g/8oz lamb neck fillet
1 tbsp soy sauce
1½ tsps sesame oil
Half a cucumber
1.14 litres/2 pints chicken stock
Salt and freshly ground black
  pepper
1½ tbsps wine vinegar

Cut the lamb into wafer thin slices then sprinkle with the soy sauce and sesame oil. Marinate for 15 minutes. Thinly slice the cucumber.

Season the stock with salt and pepper, and bring to the boil. Add the the sliced lamb and poach it in the stock for 2 minutes. Remove the meat with a slotted spoon. Poach the cucumber in the stock for 1 minute. Return the lamb, stir in the vinegar, adjust the seasoning and serve.

HOT & SOUR SOUP

Hot and Sour soup has a sharp, peppery flavour which is most unusual. Although more traditional in Thai and Vietnamese cooking, a little very finely chopped lemon grass may be added.

Serves 4

INGREDIENTS
4 Chinese dried mushrooms
120g/4oz lean pork fillet
2 tbsps sunflower or vegetable oil
60g/2oz bamboo shoots, sliced
1.14 litres/2 pints light, clear stock, or hot water plus 2 chicken stock cubes
60g/2oz tofu or bean curd, diced
1 tsp cornflour
2 tbsps cold water
1 tsp sesame oil

Marinade
1 tbsp light soy sauce
3 tbsps vinegar
2 tbsps water
1 tsp sesame oil
Salt and freshly ground black pepper

Garnish
Fresh coriander

Soak the Chinese mushrooms for 20 minutes in hot water. Meanwhile, slice the pork fillet into thin slivers. Make the marinade by combining all the ingredients together, then pour it over the pork in a bowl, and leave for 30 minutes.

Drain the mushrooms, discard the stalks and slice the caps very finely. Remove the pork from the marinade with a slotted spoon and reserve the marinade.

Heat a wok, and add the sunflower or vegetable oil. When hot, add the pork, mushrooms and bamboo shoots and stir-fry for 2 minutes. Add the stock and bring to the boil, then simmer for 10 minutes. Add the bean curd, marinade, and salt and pepper to taste. Mix the cornflour to a paste with the cold water, then add it to the soup and allow it to simmer for 5 minutes. Add the sesame oil and sprinkle with fresh coriander. Serve hot.

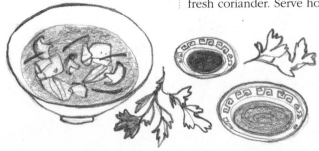

CHINESE COMBINATION SOUP

This soup combines many favourite soup ingredients in one broth; Chinese mushrooms, shredded chicken, noodles and vegetables, making a much heartier soup than most.

Serves 4

INGREDIENTS

4 Chinese dried mushrooms
120g/4oz fine thread egg noodles
225g/8oz chicken
1 tbsp peanut oil
1 clove garlic, thinly sliced
1 tsp finely chopped fresh root
   ginger
2 shallots, finely sliced
¼ small cabbage, shredded
570ml/1 pint chicken stock
2 eggs, lightly beaten
1 tsp cornflour
1 tbsp water
1 tbsp dark soy sauce
1 tbsp sherry

Soak the mushrooms in hot water for 20 minutes. Remove and discard the stalks, then slice the mushroom caps thinly. Soak the noodles in boiling salted water for 2 minutes, then rinse in cold water and drain. Slice the chicken finely.

Heat a wok and add the peanut oil. Add the garlic and ginger, and fry gently for 5 minutes, then discard the vegetables – this will just flavour the oil. Add the chicken and fry for a few minutes until the meat has turned white. Add the mushrooms, shallots, cabbage and the stock. Bring to the boil, then simmer for 5 minutes. Gradually pour in the eggs and stir so that they cook in shreds. Mix the cornflour to a paste with the water, and pour into the soup, stirring continuously. Cook for 2 minutes or until the soup boils and thickens. Add the noodles, soy sauce and sherry. Serve immediately.

FISH & RICE SOUP

The fish fillets used for this soup are cut into very fine shreds and need next-to-no cooking. Allowing them to stand in the hot soup provides all the cooking that is necessary.

Serves 4

INGREDIENTS
700ml/1¼ pints fish stock
1 tbsp soy sauce
1 slice fresh root ginger, peeled and finely chopped
340g/12oz fresh cod or haddock fillet
½ tsp cornflour, combined with a little water
120g/4oz rice, part-cooked for 8 minutes
Salt and freshly ground black pepper

Heat together the fish stock, soy sauce and ginger in a large pan. Cut the fish fillets into very thin slices and then into strips. Stir the cornflour paste into the stock and simmer gently for 10 minutes, then add the drained, part-cooked rice and cook for a further 5 minutes. Remove the pan from the heat and add the fish. Allow the fish to cook for 2-3 minutes in the hot soup. Check the seasoning, adding salt and pepper as necessary and serve immediately.

DUCK CARCASS SOUP

This soup is sometimes served after a main course of Peking Duck – it is made from the carcass and one or two simple ingredients.

Serves 4

INGREDIENTS
½ Chinese cabbage
225g/8oz tofu or bean curd
1 duck carcass
2 tbsps soy sauce
1 tbsp vinegar
1.14 litres/2 pints water

Cut the cabbage into 5cm/2 inch pieces and cut the tofu into 1.25cm/½ inch pieces. Place the duck carcass in a large pan with the cabbage, bean curd, soy sauce and vinegar. Add sufficient cold water to cover, and bring to the boil. Simmer the soup for 30 minutes, then remove the carcass and serve the soup.

SHARK'S FIN SOUP

Shark's fin is a highly prized delicacy in Chinese cookery. It is the dorsal fin of certain species of shark which is salted and then dried. This recipe uses crabmeat and chicken for flavour – the shark's fin merely adds texture to the soup.

Serves 4-6

INGREDIENTS
60g/2oz shark's fin
8 Chinese dried mushrooms
Water
3-4 slices fresh root ginger,
  peeled
1.14 litres/2 pints chicken stock
1 tsp salt
1 tbsp dark soy sauce
175g/6oz crabmeat
225g/8oz cooked chicken meat,
  shredded
2 tbsps cornflour, blended with
  5 tbsps water
3-4 tsps sesame oil

Soak the shark's fin and the dried mushrooms overnight in separate bowls of cold water. Drain the fins then place them in a saucepan with 1.14 litres/2 pints of cold water. Shred the root ginger finely and add it to the pan. Bring to the boil then simmer for 1½ hours. Drain and simmer in fresh water for a further 45 minutes, then drain again.

Drain the mushrooms, remove the stems and quarter the caps. Heat the stock in a saucepan or flameproof ceramic pot (the traditional Chinese utensil). When boiling, add the mushrooms and fins and simmer for 15 minutes. Add the salt, soy sauce and the crabmeat. Bring to the boil and boil for 2-3 minutes. Add the shredded chicken and cornflour mixture. Return the soup to the boil for a further 3-4 minutes. Sprinkle with sesame oil and serve.

WONTON SOUP WITH WATERCRESS

Wontons are often served fried but they are just as good boiled or steamed, when they may be served in soup. Make certain that you seal the edges of the wonton wrappers to completely enclose the filling.

Serves 4-6

INGREDIENTS

1 bunch watercress
225g/8oz minced pork
2 tbsps soy sauce
2 tsps sesame oil
½ tsp sugar
1 tbsp white wine
½ tsp freshly ground black pepper
½ tsp ground ginger
120g/4oz ready-made wonton wrappers
1.14 litres/2 pints chicken stock
1 tsp salt

Chop half the watercress and place it in individual soup bowls. Rinse the other half in boiling water. Drain and finely chop, then mix it with the minced pork, 1 tbsp of the soy sauce, 1 tsp of the sesame oil, the sugar, white wine, pepper and ground ginger. Marinate for 5-6 minutes.

Place half a teaspoonful of mixture just below the centre of each wonton wrapper. Fold one side over the filling. Moisten the corners with water and fold over to seal, completely enclosing the filling. Continue making wontons until all the filling mixture is used.

Bring 2.3 litres/4 pints water to the boil in a deep pan, add the wontons, return to the boil and cook for 5 minutes. Bring the chicken stock to the boil in a separate pan, and add salt and remaining soy sauce. Transfer the wontons to the soup, add the remaining sesame oil and pour the soup into the watercress lined bowls.

FISH SOUP WITH SWEETCORN

This soup may seem extravagant as the mixed fish is discarded after preparing the stock. Fish heads and bones will make a good stock and may be bought very cheaply.

Serves 4

INGREDIENTS
1 tbsp oil
1 carrot, chopped
1 onion, chopped
½ leek, chopped
1 bay leaf
1kg/2¼ lbs mixed fish
2 trout fillets
1 cod or fresh haddock fillet
2 tbsps oyster sauce
1 tbsp soy sauce
½ tsp cornflour, combined with a little water
225g/8oz sweetcorn
Salt and freshly ground black pepper

Prepare a fish stock; heat the oil in a large saucepan and gently fry the carrot, onion, leek and bay leaf. When the vegetables are lightly coloured, add the 1kg/2¼ lbs mixed fish, together with all the heads and bones. Cover with water and boil for 20 minutes. Strain through a fine sieve, reserving only the stock.

Slice the trout and cod or haddock fillets thinly and set them aside. Measure 700ml/1¼ pints of fish stock into a saucepan and bring it to the boil. Stir in the oyster sauce, soy sauce, cornflour and the sweetcorn, then boil for 10 minutes. Add the sliced fish and remove the pan from the heat. Check the seasoning, adding salt and pepper as necessary. Allow to stand for 1 minute before serving.

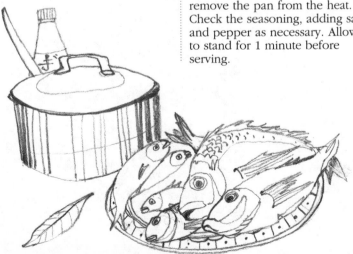

PEKING-STYLE SOUP

*Duck stock is widely used in Chinese cookery as a large
number of duck dishes are eaten, providing plenty of bones
for stock. A brown chicken stock could be used as an
alternative.*

Serves 4

INGREDIENTS
4 slices smoked ham
340g/12oz Chinese leaves
700ml/1¼ pints duck stock
1 tbsp sesame seeds
1 small clove garlic, finely
  chopped
1 tbsp soy sauce
½ tsp white wine vinegar
Salt and freshly ground black
  pepper
1 egg yolk, beaten

Cut the ham into small, evenly-
sized pieces. Cut the Chinese
leaves into small pieces and
simmer briskly for 10 minutes in
the duck stock. Stir in the sesame
seeds, garlic, ham, soy sauce,
vinegar and salt and pepper to
taste. Cook for 10 minutes over a
gentle heat. Using a teaspoon,
drizzle the beaten egg yolk into
the soup. Serve immediately.

LAMB & NOODLE SOUP

Use lamb neck fillet, thinly sliced, for this recipe. It is very lean and tender and so it will cook quickly in this soup.

Serves 4

INGREDIENTS
120g/4oz cellophane noodles
6 Chinese dried mushrooms, soaked for 15 minutes in warm water
700ml/1¼ pints lamb stock, skimmed
175g/6oz lamb fillet, thinly sliced
1 tbsp soy sauce
Few drops chilli sauce
Salt and freshly ground black pepper

Break the cellophane noodles into small pieces and cook them briefly in boiling, salted water for 20 seconds. Rinse them in fresh water and set aside to drain. Cook the mushrooms in lightly salted, boiling water for 15 minutes, then rinse them in fresh water and set aside to drain. Cut the mushrooms into thin slices.

Heat the lamb stock in a saucepan and add the lamb, mushrooms, soy sauce and a few drops of chilli sauce. Season with salt and pepper and simmer gently for 15 minutes. Stir in the drained noodles and simmer for just long enough to heat the noodles through. Serve immediately.

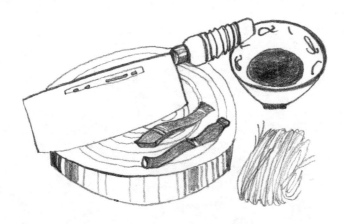

BAMBOO SHOOT SOUP

This is an elegant soup, elegant in flavour and in presentation. The strands of sieved egg provide a very decorative garnish.

Serves 4

INGREDIENTS

120g/4oz bamboo shoots, cut into thin matchsticks
4 Chinese dried black mushrooms, soaked for 15 minutes in warm water
700ml/1¼ pints chicken stock
1 tbsp wine vinegar
2 tbsps light soy sauce
Salt and freshly ground black pepper
½ tsp cornflour, combined with a little water
1 egg, beaten
10 chives, chopped

Blanch the bamboo shoots in boiling, salted water for 3 minutes. Rinse and set aside to drain. Cook the mushrooms in boiling, salted water for 10 minutes. Rinse and set aside to drain.

Bring the stock to the boil in a large saucepan and add the bamboo shoots, mushrooms, vinegar and soy sauce and season with salt and pepper to taste. Cook for 10 minutes. Stir in the cornflour paste and bring the soup slowly back to the boil, then reduce the heat. Place the beaten egg in a sieve and add to the soup by shaking the sieve back and forth over the hot soup - the egg will set in strands almost immediately. Add the chives to the soup and serve piping hot.

CLEAR CHICKEN SOUP WITH EGG

Do not overcook the eggs when poaching or they will be tough and rubbery in the soup. Use a good home-made chicken stock in this soup for the very best results.

Serves 4

INGREDIENTS
4 Chinese dried mushrooms, soaked for 15 minutes in warm water
1 tbsp coarse sea salt
1 tbsp wine vinegar
1 bay leaf.
4 eggs
700ml/1¼ pints chicken stock
1 onion, chopped
Salt and freshly ground black pepper
10 chives, chopped
1 tbsp soy sauce
Few drops chilli sauce

Cook the mushrooms in boiling, salted water for 15 minutes, rinse in fresh water and set aside to drain. Discard any hard stalks and cut the caps into thin slices. Bring a large saucepan of water to the boil with the sea salt, vinegar and bay leaf. Reduce the heat to a gentle simmer and carefully break the eggs into the water one at a time. Poach the eggs for 1 minute and then remove them from the boiling water with a slotted spoon. Drain the eggs on a clean tea-towel.

Bring the stock to the boil in a saucepan with the onion, then simmer for 10 minutes. Strain through a fine sieve, discarding the onion. Check the seasoning, adding salt and pepper as necessary. Bring the stock back to the boil and add the mushrooms, chives, soy sauce and a few drops of chilli sauce. Cook for 10 minutes. One minute before serving add the eggs.

FISH SOUP WITH
SURPRISE WONTONS

*This soup is lightly flavoured with prawns and soy sauce. The
wontons are filled with stir-fried garlic prawns and make
explosive mouthfuls of flavour in an otherwise plain soup.*

Serves 4

INGREDIENTS
700ml/1¼ pints fish stock
12 fresh prawns, peeled and
  heads removed; peelings and
  heads set aside
1 tbsp oil
½ tsp freshly chopped parsley
1 small clove garlic, finely
  chopped
Salt and freshly ground black
  pepper
12 wonton wrappers
1 egg, beaten
1 tbsp soy sauce

Bring the fish stock to the boil,
together with the reserved heads
and peelings from the prawns,
then simmer gently for 15
minutes. Strain through a fine
sieve, reserving only the stock.
Chop 4 of the prawns. Heat the
oil in a wok and stir-fry the

chopped prawns together with
the parsley, garlic and salt and
pepper to taste. Allow to cool.

Spread out the wonton wrappers
and place a little of the prawn
stuffing on each one. Brush the
beaten egg all around the edges
of the dough. Fold one side over
on to the other, cut the wontons
into the desired shape and seal
well by pinching the edges
together firmly. Set aside to rest
for 10 minutes.

Return the stock to the boil, then
add the remaining prawns and
the soy sauce. Pinch once more
round the edges of the wontons,
then slip them into the stock.
Season with salt and pepper and
simmer briskly for 5 minutes.
Serve piping hot.

CHICKEN & BEAN SPROUT SOUP

An ideal soup to make with left-over meat from a cooked chicken, this is quick to prepare and aromatic to the senses.

Serves 4

INGREDIENTS
225g/8oz cooked chicken
340g/12oz bean sprouts
700ml/1¼ pints chicken stock
1 tbsp white wine vinegar
2 tsps sugar
2 tbsps soy sauce
1 tbsp chopped onion
2 shallots, chopped
Salt and freshly ground black
  pepper

Cut the chicken into small dice. Place the bean sprouts and stock in a saucepan and bring to the boil. Reduce the heat and add the chicken, vinegar, sugar, soy sauce, onion, shallots and salt and pepper to taste. Stir well and simmer the soup for 15 minutes over a moderate heat. Serve hot.

BEEF & NOODLE SOUP

*It seems very extravagant to use fillet steak for a soup!
However, with the noodles and seasonings this makes a very
rich and filling soup and is almost a meal in itself.*

Serves 4

INGREDIENTS

225g/8oz fillet of beef
1 large clove garlic, finely
  chopped
1 spring onion, chopped
2 tbsps soy sauce
Salt and freshly ground black
  pepper
225g/8oz fresh egg noodles or
  thin pasta
Few drops sesame oil
700ml/1¼ pints beef stock
Few drops chilli sauce
1 tbsp freshly chopped chives

Cut the beef into thin slices, and sprinkle with the chopped garlic and spring onion. Sprinkle over the soy sauce and season with salt and pepper. Leave the meat to marinate for 15 minutes.

Cook the noodles in boiling, salted water to which a few drops of sesame oil have been added. Rinse them in cold water and set aside to drain. Bring the stock to the boil and add the beef and the marinade. Simmer gently for 10 minutes. Stir in the noodles, season with a few drops of chilli sauce and simmer for just long enough to heat the noodles through. Serve with the chives sprinkled over the top.

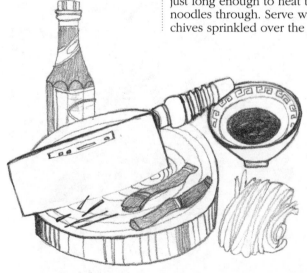

TURKEY SOUP WITH BLACK MUSHROOMS

Frying the turkey in sesame oil gives a delightful fragrance to what can otherwise be rather a bland meat. The mushrooms and ginger combine for extra seasoning in this soup which may be made economically at any time of year.

Serves 4

INGREDIENTS
175g/6oz turkey breast
1 tbsp sesame oil
60g/2oz Chinese dried black
   mushrooms, soaked for 15
   minutes in warm water
700ml/1¼ pints chicken stock
1 tbsp soy sauce
1 slice fresh root ginger, peeled
   and finely chopped
Salt and freshly ground black
   pepper

Cut the turkey meat into slices and then into small cubes. Heat the sesame oil in a wok and stir-fry the meat until browned. Remove from the pan with a slotted spoon and drain off all the excess oil from the wok. Cook the mushrooms in boiling, salted water for 10 minutes. Rinse and drain well. Place the mushrooms in a saucepan with the stock. Stir in the turkey, soy sauce, ginger and salt and pepper to taste. Bring to the boil and then simmer gently for 15 minutes. Serve the soup piping hot.

RICE SOUP

This is a simple and economical soup to make and is a good way of using up left-over meat; any meat or chicken may be used. The rice makes the soup just a little more substantial.

Serves 4

INGREDIENTS

4 Chinese dried mushrooms, soaked in warm water for 15 minutes
700ml/1¼ pints duck stock
1 spring onion, chopped
2 tbsps sweetcorn
120g/4oz cooked meat, finely diced
Pinch of ground ginger
1 tbsp rice wine
1 tbsp soy sauce
Salt and freshly ground black pepper
120g/4oz cooked rice

Drain the mushrooms and slice them thinly, discarding the stalks. Place them in a saucepan with the stock and spring onion, then add the sweetcorn, meat, ginger, rice wine, soy sauce, and salt and pepper to taste. Bring to the boil and simmer briskly for 10 minutes. Stir in the rice and cook for 1 minute. Check the seasoning, adjust as necessary, and serve.

ABALONE SOUP

Abalone is one of those foods, like balsamic vinegar, which has suddenly become very popular in many parts of the world. Abalone are molluscs, about 12.5cm/5 inches in diameter, and it is the muscle that is eaten – so it can be tough. Although popular in Oriental cooking abalone are also found in the Channel Islands and in parts of America. The European abalone is smaller than other varieties. Fresh abalone should be beaten to tenderise them – canned ones do not need this rough treatment!

Serves 4

INGREDIENTS
700ml/1¼ pints fish stock
6 canned abalone plus 2 tbsps
   reserved juice
½ spring onion, chopped
1 tbsp soy sauce
2 tsps oyster sauce
1 egg white
Salt and freshly ground black
   pepper

Heat together the fish stock, the reserved abalone juice, spring onion, soy sauce and oyster sauce. Cut the canned abalone first into thin slices and then into matchsticks. Add to the stock and simmer gently for 15 minutes. Beat the egg white lightly and then stir it gradually into the boiling soup. Season with salt and pepper to taste and serve.

CHICKEN & SWEETCORN SOUP

I think Chicken & Sweetcorn is probably the most popular Chinese soup in western restaurants. A little fresh ginger makes it very special.

Serves 4

INGREDIENTS
175g/6oz sweetcorn
700ml/1¼ pints chicken stock
2 cooked chicken breasts
12 baby sweetcorns
2.5cm/1 inch piece fresh root ginger, peeled and finely chopped
2 tbsps light soy sauce
Pinch of monosodium glutamate (optional)
Few drops chilli sauce
Salt and freshly ground black pepper

Place the sweetcorn in a liquidiser or food processor with 120ml/4 fl oz of the chicken stock and blend until smooth. Strain the purée through a sieve, pushing it through with the back of a spoon.

Cut the cooked chicken into thin slices and place it in a saucepan with the remaining stock. Stir in the sweetcorn purée, and add the baby corns then bring to the boil. Simmer for 15 minutes. Add the ginger, soy sauce, and monosodium glutamate, if using. Continue cooking for another 10 minutes, then add a few drops of chilli sauce. Check the seasoning, adding salt and pepper if necesary, and serve.

CRAB SOUP WITH GINGER

This luxurious soup is very special and suitable for even the most lavish entertaining. Shaohsing wine is rice wine; dry sherry could be used in its place. If you are using fresh crabmeat and not cooking your own crabs, you merely need to combine the crabmeat with the well-flavoured fish stock, ginger and sake and heat the soup before seasoning to taste.

Serves 4

INGREDIENTS

1 carrot, chopped
1 onion, chopped
½ leek, chopped
1 bay leaf
2 medium-sized fresh crabs or 280g/10oz fresh crabmeat
700ml/1¼ pints fish stock
2.5cm/1 inch piece of fresh root ginger, peeled and chopped
1 tsp Shaohsing wine
Salt and freshly ground black pepper

Make a vegetable stock by placing the carrot, onion, leek and bay leaf in a saucepan with a large quantity of water. Bring to the boil and add the crabs. Allow them to boil briskly for 20 minutes or until cooked. Remove the crabs and allow them to cool. Once cooled, break off the pincers and break the joints, cut open the back and open the claws. Carefully remove all the crabmeat, discarding the dead men's fingers. Bring the fish stock to the boil and add the ginger, Shaohsing wine and the crabmeat. Boil for 15 minutes. Check the seasoning, adding salt and pepper as necessary. Serve very hot.

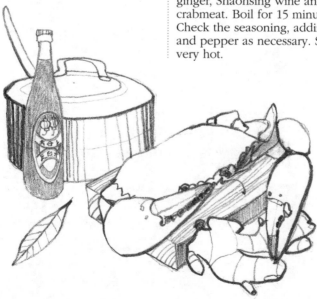

WONTON SOUP

Wonton is to the Chinese what ravioli pasta is to the Italians – a means of enclosing a filling for serving in a soup or a sauce. Prepared wonton wrappers are available in specialist food shops.

Serves 6-8

INGREDIENTS
20-24 wonton wrappers
90g/3oz finely minced chicken or pork
2 tbsps freshly chopped Chinese parsley or coriander
3 spring onions, finely chopped
2.5cm/1 inch piece fresh root ginger, peeled and grated
1 egg, lightly beaten
1.4 litres/2½ pints chicken stock
1 tbsp dark soy sauce
Few drops sesame oil
Salt and freshly ground black pepper
Chinese parsley or watercress for garnish

Place all the wonton wrappers on a large, flat surface. Mix together the chicken or pork, chopped Chinese parsley, spring onions and ginger. Brush the edges of the wrappers lightly with beaten egg. Place a small mound of mixture on one half of each wrapper and fold the other half over the top to form a triangle. Press well to seal the edges.

Bring the stock to the boil in a large saucepan. Add the filled wontons and simmer for 5-10 minutes or until they float to the surface. Add all the remaining ingredients to the soup, using only the leaves of the Chinese parsley or watercress for garnish.

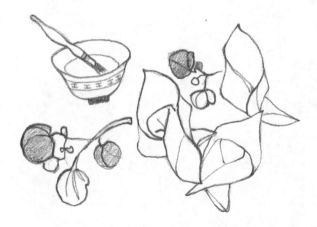

CRAB & SWEETCORN SOUP

Crab and sweetcorn make a creamy, fragrant combination of flavours for this soup – I sometimes use ocean sticks (which are not traditional!) but you can't beat the flavour of fresh crabmeat.

Serves 4-6

INGREDIENTS
1 litre/1¾ pints fish or chicken
   stock
340g/12oz creamed sweetcorn
120g/4oz crabmeat
Salt and freshly ground black
   pepper
1 tsp light soy sauce
2 tbsps cornflour
3 tbsps water or stock
2 egg whites, whisked
4 spring onions for garnish

Bring the stock to the boil in a large pan. Add the sweetcorn, crabmeat, seasonings and soy sauce, then allow to simmer for 4-5 minutes. Mix the cornflour and water or stock and add a spoonful of the hot soup. Add the mixture to the soup and return it to the boil. Cook until the soup thickens. Whisk the egg whites until soft peaks form. Stir into the hot soup just before serving. Slice the onions thinly on the diagonal and scatter over the top to garnish.

STARTERS & APPETISERS

I could easily stop here and say that these never happen! Well, in the typical way of serving a Chinese meal, any dish that we would consider to be suitable for an appetiser would just be included in a buffet-style meal! It has really just been to satisfy the Western restaurant trade that some classic Chinese dishes have been labelled as starters and are served as such, to help us feel that we are having a 'proper' meal!

Starters, Snacks and Teahouses
Many Chinese dishes are perfect finger food and, as such, make wonderful cocktail nibbles, drinks party snacks and finger food

for relaxed and informal entertaining. Such dishes have been enjoyed in China for hundreds of years, but were originally limited to the members of the Imperial Household who had their chefs prepare the snacks for eating throughout the day. They gradually found their way into all Chinese diets and became very popular.

The Chinese would regard these more as teahouse dishes. Snacks are served in teahouses all day and one is more likely to nibble at small quantities of a vast number of foods, rather than having a formal meal. They can be quite time-consuming to prepare and might therefore be better suited to eating out than preparing at home. Steamed buns, spring rolls and prawn toasts would all be found on a teahouse menu, and the variety of foods far outnumbers the number of drinks on offer, including teas and wines.

Order 'What You Fancy'

'A little of what you fancy does you good' – well, that's a good rule for life but it is so often an excuse for over-indulgence! Many western restaurant menus now include a starter called 'Dim Sum' which literally means eating snacks for pleasure or order what you fancy! Whenever I order this I receive a selection of three or four starters or snacks, including tiny spring rolls, miniature pork dumplings which are often steamed, and a few small pieces of spare ribs – an ideal starter!

As dim sum have become more popular many restaurants specialising in these foods have opened up, mainly in America and Hong Kong, pandering to the western taste for savoury snacks. There is such a variety of dim sum that you can easily make a complete meal out of ten or twelve varieties.

The recipes that I have selected for this chapter of suggested Chinese starters are not the most complicated of the dim sum recipes, but are those which may easily be prepared at home. Some ingredients that we might be tempted to ignore make excellent finger food – chicken wings are virtually impossible to eat decorously with a knife and fork but, coated in honey and soy, they make a delicious Chinese appetiser.

Spring Rolls – the All-time Favourite

Spring Rolls are probably the most popular of all the Chinese starters or snacks. They can be served plain, or with a sweet

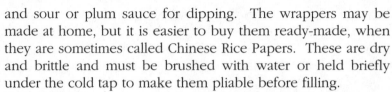

and sour or plum sauce for dipping. The wrappers may be made at home, but it is easier to buy them ready-made, when they are sometimes called Chinese Rice Papers. These are dry and brittle and must be brushed with water or held briefly under the cold tap to make them pliable before filling.

Spring Rolls may contain small amounts of shredded chicken or pork, or even a little shellfish, but the main filling ingredients are vegetables, especially bean sprouts. These do not require chopping if you are making large rolls to be eaten over a plate, but if you are making smaller rolls to serve as finger food, chop the filling so that it will be possible to bite through the roll without embarrassment!

Spring rolls are always deep fried. Drain well on absorbent kitchen paper before serving.

Spare Ribs in the Oriental Style

Spare ribs have always been a popular dish in China but they have also enjoyed enormous success in restaurants around the world. Served outside China the ribs are often very large, more like American ribs, but in China they are cut into much smaller pieces, about 5cm/2 inches long and are much more delicate (and easier) to eat.

As Chinese starters are predominantly finger food ensure that you offer finger bowls or hot flannels to all those sharing the meal, so that they can clean up, ready for the next course!

CRAB ROLLS

Crab Rolls are prepared in exactly the same way as spring rolls. Make certain that the filling is totally enclosed by the spring roll wrappers; the outside will become crispy while the filling remains succulently moist.

Serves 4

INGREDIENTS
30g/1oz cellophane noodles
175g/6oz crabmeat, fresh or
 canned
3 spring onions, finely sliced
½ tsp grated fresh root ginger
2 tbsps finely chopped bamboo
 shoots
1 tsp oyster sauce
Salt
12 spring roll wrappers
Vegetable or peanut oil for deep-
 frying

Soak the cellophane noodles in hot water for 8 minutes, or as directed on the packet, then drain. Flake the crabmeat, draining if necessary, then mix it with the spring onions, noodles, ginger, bamboo shoots, oyster sauce, and salt to taste. Place the spring roll wrappers on a work surface with a corner pointing towards you. Place a little of the filling just below the centre of each. Fold the bottom corner over the filling then fold in the two sides. Roll up, completely enclosing the filling and damping the edges to seal the rolls – a flour and water paste may be used if necessary. Refrigerate the rolls if they are not to be cooked immediately.

Heat some oil in a wok and deep-fry the crab rolls, four at a time. Drain on absorbent kitchen paper. Serve warm with ginger sauce or sweet-and-sour sauce.

RICE-COATED MEATBALLS

This recipe suggests using minced pork, but chicken, turkey, beef or lamb could be used with equally good results.

Serves 4

INGREDIENTS
225g/8oz boned pork shoulder, minced
2.5cm/1 inch piece fresh root ginger, peeled and chopped
½ tsp shallot, finely chopped
½ tsp freshly chopped parsley
½ tsp freshly chopped chives
½ tsp soy sauce
½ egg, beaten
Few drops chilli sauce
Salt and freshly ground black pepper
120g/4oz long grain rice, pre-soaked in warm water for 2 hours

Mix the meat, ginger, shallots, parsley, chives, soy sauce, egg and chilli sauce. Beat well to combine all the ingredients. Season with salt and pepper and then form into small meat balls. Drain the rice very carefully, shaking well to remove all the water. Spread the rice over a work surface. Roll the meat balls in the rice to coat them evenly. Steam the meat balls for 15 minutes or until cooked. The exact cooking time will depend on the thickness of your meatballs, but small ones take 15 minutes.

RICE PAPER PRAWN PARCELS

Chinese rice papers are not to be confused with the thick European variety used as a base for macaroons! They are thin, brittle, almost translucent circles made from a paste of rice flour and water and must be softened with water before being filled.

Serves 4

INGREDIENTS
225g/8oz prawns or shrimps, shelled and de-veined
1 egg white
½ tsp cornflour
1 tsp Chinese wine or 2 tsps dry sherry
1 tsp sugar
1 tsp light soy sauce
6 spring onions, sliced finely
Salt and freshly ground black pepper
1 packet Chinese rice papers
150ml/¼ pint peanut oil

Dry the prepared prawns on absorbent kitchen paper. Mix the egg white, cornflour, wine, sugar, soy sauce, spring onions and seasoning together, then mix in the prawns. Heat the peanut oil in a wok until hot. Soften the rice papers by brushing them or dipping them in water – this makes them more manageable. Wrap five or six prawns in each piece of dampened rice paper. Gently drop the rice paper parcels into hot oil and deep-fry for about 5 minutes. Serve hot.

SPRING ROLLS

Spring rolls make a popular starter but are also sometimes served to accompany a main course. Both the wrapper and the enclosed vegetables should be crispy.

Serves 4-6

INGREDIENTS

Wrappers
120g/4oz strong plain flour
1 egg, beaten
Cold water

Filling
225g/8oz pork, trimmed and
   finely shredded
120g/4oz prawns, shelled and
   chopped
4 spring onions, finely chopped
2 tsps chopped fresh root ginger
120g/4oz Chinese leaves,
   shredded
100g/3½oz bean sprouts
1 tbsp light soy sauce
Dash sesame oil
1 egg, beaten
Oil for deep-frying

To prepare the wrappers, sift the flour into a bowl and make a well in the centre. Add the beaten egg and about 1 tbsp cold water. Begin beating with a wooden spoon, gradually drawing in the flour to make a smooth dough. Add more water if necessary. Knead the dough until it is elastic and pliable. Place in a covered bowl and chill for about 4 hours or overnight. Allow the dough to come back to room temperature before rolling out – this will take about 20-30 minutes.

Flour a large work surface well and roll the dough out until 6mm/¼ inch thick. Cut the dough into 12 equal squares and then roll each piece into a larger square about 15 × 15cm/6 × 6 inches. The dough should be very thin. Cover the dough while preparing the filling.

Cook the pork in 1-2 tbsps of the frying oil for about 2-3 minutes. Add the remaining filling ingredients, except the beaten egg, and cook for a further 2-3 minutes, then allow to cool.

Lay out the wrappers on a clean work surface with the point of each wrapper towards you. Brush the edges lightly with the beaten egg. Divide the filling between the 12 wrappers, placing it just above the front point. Fold over the sides like an envelope, then fold over the point until the filling is completely covered. Roll up as for a Swiss roll, and press all the edges together to seal well.

Heat the oil in a deep fat fryer or in a deep pan to 190°C/375°F. Depending on the size of the fryer, add 2-4 spring rolls at a time and fry until golden brown on both sides. The rolls will float to the surface when one side has browned and they should be turned over. Drain thoroughly on absorbent kitchen paper and serve hot.

PRAWN TOASTS

This is one of my favourite Oriental 'starters'. I sometimes serve a chilli and cucumber dressing with the toasts which are light, savoury and delicious.

Serves 4-6 as a starter

INGREDIENTS
225g/8oz prawns or shrimps, shelled, de-veined, and finely chopped
1 small egg, beaten
2 tsps sherry
2 tsps oyster sauce
½ tsp grated fresh root ginger
2 tsp cornflour
Salt
5 slices white bread
Oil for deep-frying

Combine the prawns in a bowl with the beaten egg, sherry, oyster sauce, grated ginger, cornflour and a pinch of salt.

Using a 4cm/1½ inch round pastry cutter, cut out circles of bread. Spread a little of the prawn mixture on each, making sure that all the bread is well covered. Heat the oil in a wok for deep-frying. Fry the toasts in batches with the bread side uppermost, until the bread is golden brown. Remove the toasts with a slotted spoon and drain on absorbent kitchen paper. Keep hot until all the toasts are cooked.

IMPERIAL PORK ROLLS

These crispy pork rolls are dipped into a spicy sauce before being eaten. This is finger food, so you may like to wrap the Imperial Pork Rolls in lettuce leaves to stop your fingers becoming too greasy.

Serves 4

INGREDIENTS
Dipping Sauce
2 tsps vinegar
1 tbsp water
1 tbsp fish sauce
1 tsp sugar
½ tsp finely chopped fresh root
ginger
Chilli sauce

Pork Rolls
4 Chinese dried black
mushrooms, soaked for 15
minutes in warm water
340g/12oz boneless shoulder of
pork, very finely chopped
½ tsp oil
120g/4oz bean sprouts, blanched
and drained
1 tbsp soy sauce
½ tsp cornflour
Salt and freshly ground black
pepper
16 sheets Chinese rice paper,
soaked in warm water for 10
minutes
1 egg, beaten
120ml/4 fl oz oil

Prepare the sauce; mix together the vinegar, water, fish sauce, sugar and ginger and allow to stand for 30 minutes. Add a few drops of chilli sauce, just before serving.

Dice the mushrooms very finely and mix them with the pork. Heat the ½ tsp of oil in a wok and stir-fry the mushrooms and pork with the bean sprouts, soy sauce and cornflour for 2 minutes. Allow to cool. The mixture should be quite dry. Add salt, pepper and chilli sauce to taste.

Drain the rice paper sheets and spread them out on your work surface. Place a little of the cooled stuffing in the centre of each sheet, roll it up and seal the edges with a little of the beaten egg.

Heat the remaining oil in a wok and fry the pork rolls gently on all sides, beginning with the sealed side. Drain on absorbent kitchen paper. Serve the rolls hot, with the dipping sauce in individual bowls.

CROUTON STUDDED 'POMEGRANATE' CRISPY PRAWN BALLS

These 'spiky' prawn balls make a good starter or may also be served as cocktail nibbles or finger food. Cut the croutons very small so that they will stick to the prawn balls. Serve with stir-fired vegetables as a main course.

Serves 4

INGREDIENTS
4 slices white bread
225g/8oz white fish fillets
225g/8oz prawns, fresh or frozen
2 tsps salt
Freshly ground black pepper to taste
2 egg whites
2 slices fresh root ginger, peeled and finely chopped
2 tbsps cornflour
Oil for deep-frying

Remove the crusts from the bread, then cut each slice into tiny cubes. Dry in a hot oven until slightly browned then spread the croutons out on a large tray. Chop the fish and shelled prawns very finely, then mix them with the salt, pepper, egg white, finely chopped ginger, and cornflour. Blend well. Shape the mixture into 5cm/2 inch balls. Roll over the dried bread croutons to coat the prawn balls.

Heat the oil in a deep-fryer or wok. Add the crouton studded prawn balls one by one. Turn with a slotted spoon until evenly browned, in about 2 minutes. Remove and drain on absorbent kitchen paper. Return to the oil and cook for a further 1 minute. Drain well on absorbent kitchen paper. Serve with good quality soy sauce, ketchup and chilli sauce as dips.

CHINESE OMELETTE

This is a substantial omelette filled with chicken, ham and prawns. It will serve four people as a starter or two people as a light main course.

Serves 4

INGREDIENTS
8 eggs, beaten
2 slices ham, chopped
175g/6oz cooked chicken meat
8 cooked prawns, peeled and
   chopped
1 tbsp freshly chopped chives
2 tsps soy sauce
Salt and freshly ground black
   pepper
2 tbsps oil

Mix together the eggs, ham, chicken and prawns in a bowl. Stir in the chives and soy sauce and check the seasoning, adding salt and pepper to taste. Heat the oil in a frying pan and add the omelette mixture. Gently stir the omelette with a fork as it is cooking. Fold over first one side of the omelette and then the other and serve hot in slices.

HONEY SOY
CHICKEN WINGS

Do not disregard chicken wings – they make the most delicious finger food. Honey Soy Chicken Wings may be served as part of a meal or as nibbles with drinks; either way, have plenty of napkins or warm flannels ready for sticky fingers.

Serves 4

INGREDIENTS
2 tbsps peanut oil
460g/1lb chicken wings
4 tbsps light soy sauce
2 tbsps clear honey
1 tsp sesame seeds
1 clove garlic, crushed
1 tsp grated fresh root ginger
½ tsp salt

Heat a wok, add the oil and, when hot, add the chicken wings and fry for 10 minutes. Carefully strain off any excess oil. Add the soy sauce, honey, sesame seeds, garlic, grated ginger and salt to the chicken in the wok. Reduce the heat, and simmer for 20 minutes, turning the chicken wings occasionally. Serve hot or cold.

SESAME CHICKEN WINGS

Any recipe using chicken wings is economical to prepare as they are relatively cheap to buy. Hopeless to attempt to eat with a knife and fork, this is real finger food!

Serves 8

INGREDIENTS
12 chicken wings
1 tbsp salted black beans
1 tbsp water
1 tbsp oil
2 cloves garlic, crushed
2 slices fresh root ginger, peeled and cut into fine shreds
3 tbsps soy sauce
1½ tbsps dry sherry or rice wine
Large pinch of freshly ground black pepper
1 tbsp sesame seeds

Using a sharp, heavy knife, cut off and discard the wing tips, then cut through the joint and separate the wing into two pieces. Crush the beans and add the water. Leave to stand for a few minutes.

Heat the oil in a wok and add the garlic and ginger. Stir briefly and add the chicken wings. Cook, stirring, until the chicken is lightly browned, in about 3 minutes. Add the soy sauce and wine and stir-fry for a further 30 seconds. Add the soaked black beans and pepper.

Cover the wok tightly and simmer for about 8-10 minutes. Uncover and turn the heat to high. Continue stirring until the liquid is almost evaporated and the chicken wings are glazed with the sauce. Remove from the heat and sprinkle with the sesame seeds, stirring to coat the wings completely. Serve, garnished with spring onions or Chinese parsley, if wished.

QUICK FRY
'CRYSTAL PRAWNS'

This recipe is very quick to prepare, is light in flavour and not too spicy. Sprinkling the vinegar over the prawns at the last moment really helps to bring out their flavour.

Serves 4

INGREDIENTS
460g/1lb fresh prawns
1 egg white
1 tbsp cornflour
6 tbsps oil
1 tsp finely chopped fresh root ginger
2 tsps chopped onion
½ tsp salt
1 tbsp pale dry sherry
2 tbsps stock, fish, vegetable or chicken
2 tsps vinegar

Clean, shell and de-vein the prawns. Mix together the egg white and cornflour, add the prawns and coat well. Heat the oil in a wok, add the prawns and stir-fry over a low heat for 2-3 minutes until changing colour. Remove the prawns with a slotted spoon. Pour off any excess oil from the wok, then add the chopped ginger, onion, salt, sherry and stock and bring to the boil. Return the prawns to the wok and stir over the heat for a few seconds until hot. Sprinkle with vinegar and serve.

BARBECUED SPARERIBS

This is real finger-food – there is no delicate way of eating spareribs! Have plenty of finger bowls or warm flannels at the ready for sticky fingers.

Serves 4-6

INGREDIENTS
4-6 spring onions for garnish
1.8kg/4lbs pork spareribs
3 tbsps dark soy sauce
6 tbsps hoisin sauce (Chinese barbecue sauce)
2 tbsps dry sherry
¼ tsp five-spice powder
1 tbsp brown sugar

First prepare the garnish. Trim the roots and the dark green tops from the onions. Cut both ends into thin strips, leaving about 1.25cm/½ inch in the middle uncut. Place the onions in iced water for several hours or overnight so that the ends curl up.

Cut the spareribs into single ribs, if the butcher has not already done so. Mix all the remaining ingredients together, pour over the ribs and stir to coat evenly. Leave to marinade for 1 hour.

Preheat the oven to 180°C/350°F/Gas Mark 4. Place the sparerib pieces on a rack in a roasting pan containing 570ml/1 pint water, then cook in the preheated oven for 30 minutes. Add more hot water to the pan while cooking, if necessary.

Turn the ribs over and brush with the remaining sauce. Cook for a further 30 minutes or until tender. Serve garnished with the spring onions.

CARAMELIZED SPARERIBS

The honey in the sauce will caramelise on the spare ribs, giving them a sweet flavour and a lovely sticky glaze. Do keep an eye on the ribs during cooking and turn them if they start to brown too much.

Serves 4

INGREDIENTS
1 carrot
1 bay leaf
1 leek
900g/2lbs pork spareribs, separated
1 tbsp honey
1 tbsp white wine vinegar
1 tsp chopped garlic
2 tbsps soy sauce
60ml/2 fl oz chicken stock
Salt and freshly ground black pepper

Preheat the oven to 240°C/475°F/Gas Mark 9. Place 2 litres/3½ pints of water in a large saucepan with the carrot, leek and bay leaf. Bring to the boil and add the spareribs. Blanch the meat for 10 minutes, then remove the ribs from the pan and drain well. Lay the ribs in an ovenproof dish. Combine the honey, vinegar and garlic, and spread the mixture on the ribs. Add the soy sauce and chicken stock to the dish. Season well with salt and pepper.

Cook in the preheated oven for 20 minutes, or until the ribs have caramelized and turned a rich, dark brown colour.

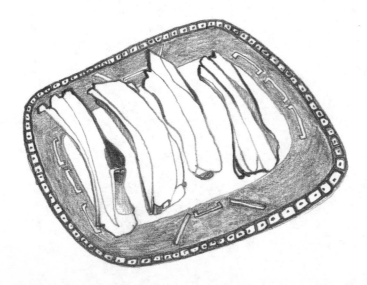

FRIED CHINESE RAVIOLI WITH SALMON

Wontons are very similar to Italian ravioli – little parcels of dough which may be filled with countless stuffings. These contain fresh salmon and chives – delicious! As they are fried they require no sauce – boiled ravioli always needs sauce.

Serves 4

INGREDIENTS
250g/9oz fresh salmon, boned, filleted and finely chopped
1 tbsp freshly chopped chives
1 squeeze lemon juice
Salt and freshly ground black pepper
24 wonton wrappers
1 egg, beaten
Oil for deep-frying

Mix the salmon with the chives, lemon juice, salt and pepper. Lay out 12 wonton wrappers and divide the stuffing evenly between them, placing it in the centre of each wrapper. Brush the beaten egg around the edges of the stuffing and top with the remaining 12 wrappers. Cut each ravioli into the desired shape and seal the edges firmly by pinching with your fingers or pushing down with a fork. Set aside to rest for 15 minutes.

Heat the oil to 170°C/340°F. Cook the wonton ravioli a few at a time in the hot oil. Remove when cooked and drain on absorbent kitchen paper. Season with salt and pepper and serve immediately.

CRISPY WONTON SAUCE

Wonton skins are available in Chinese supermarkets. They are usually filled with spiced minced pork or dried shrimps, but you could experiment with your own fillings. Deep-fry the wontons until crispy.

The wontons should be dipped in a sauce for eating. This same sauce may be used for dipping any finger foods.

INGREDIENTS
1 tbsp cornflour
1 tbsp tomato purée
1 tbsp vinegar
1 tbsp soy sauce
2 tbsps sugar
1½ tbsps oil

Place all the sauce ingredients in a pan and stir together over a medium heat for 4-5 minutes.

FISH &
SHELLFISH

Fish and shellfish play an important role in Chinese cookery and I have heard that there are at least two hundred varieties of fish in common use! The recipes in this chapter concentrate on the few most popular varieties in use throughout the country.

Fish from River and Sea
China's coastline provides wonderful fish and especially shellfish, although the marine fishing industry is relatively undeveloped. Lobster, crab, scallops and mussels are all freely available, although sea fish only accounts for about one quarter

of the total catch each year. In refreshing contrast to the coastal waters of so many other countries, the Chinese fishing grounds are relatively under-fished.

The majority of fish eaten in China comes either from the rivers or from fish farms. The latter is not a new concept – carp have been farmed for many years in special pools and this technique is now being used for a variety of species. The fish farms are often situated close to major cities as it is considered of utmost importance that no more than three or four hours should pass between the killing and the eating of the fish. It is quite common for live fish to be sold in markets in China.

China has two major rivers, the Yangtze and the Hwang Ho or Yellow River, and numerous smaller waterways, lakes and canals. They all provide numerous varieties of fish, and bream, bass and trout are widely available and very popular.

Fish as Meat!

The main advantage of fish is that it is even quicker to cook than meat! Many Chinese dishes treat it in quite a robust way, serving it in a well-flavoured sauce which might mask a delicate flavour. I like to cook strong, gamy fish such as red mullet in this way and to attempt to preserve the more delicate flavours of other fish in milder dishes.

Fish requires only light cooking. For example, although prawns or other fish may be served deep-fried with a sweet and sour or chilli sauce, the sauce will be poured over the fish balls just before serving. Fried meat cooked in the same way, is usually simmered in the sauce for a short time before serving.

Brush up your Filleting Skills

The Chinese are very fond of preparing and cooking whole fish, often by steaming. Shreds of fresh root ginger and spring onions are scattered over the fish for flavouring and a spicy sauce, prepared in a separate pan during the steaming, will be served to accompany the fish. Steamed Fish in Ginger is an example of a whole fish, stuffed, then steamed. You will need a heat-proof plate that will fit inside a steamer to cook in this way. It is also a good idea to brush up on your fish filleting skills if you are to remove the fillets neatly from the bones for serving, although large pieces of fish served on a bed of stir-fried vegetables or noodles do look very attractive. I love

serving trout in this way as the pink flesh looks really appetising.

Fresh is Best

The Chinese always pay particular attention to the freshness of their fish and this also applies to shellfish. They would always use uncooked prawns and shellfish, cooking even their own crabs and lobsters just before use. Many westerners would not do this and therefore the use of prepared or canned crabmeat has crept into recipes adapted for the western kitchen. It is now possible to buy uncooked prawns in fishmongers and supermarkets and these have a much brighter flavour than those which have been cooked and frozen. Do try them – they are a little more expensive than the cooked prawns but the flavour is well worth the expense.

Abalone – the New Fish of the Orient

Abalone have recently become popular in the west where they are wrongly regarded as an eastern delicacy. Yes, they are widely used in Chinese cookery, but there are also smaller varieties of abalone freely available in Europe and on the west coast of America. In fact, they are so common in Guernsey that there are walls covered in abalone shells!

Abalone are a variety of shellfish, a mollusc similar to a mussel. The part which is eaten is the muscle which holds the shell closed and consequently it tends to be rather tough and chewy. Abalone may be bought fresh or canned. I actually think that the canning process does slightly soften or tenderise the fish – perhaps abalone are the exception to the rule that fresh is best?

DEEP-FRIED SEA BASS

In this recipe the bass is partly cooked by frying and then finished in a tangy, spicy sauce. Rinse the pickled cabbage under running water before adding it to the dish.

Serves 4

INGREDIENTS
680g/1½lbs sea bass
3 tsps dark soy sauce
2 tbsps cornflour
850ml/1½ pints oil
60g/2oz minced pork
2 cloves garlic
2 small chillies
2 spring onions
1 slice fresh root ginger, peeled
570ml/1 pint chicken stock
2 tsps salt
90g/3oz pickled cabbage,
  shredded
2 tsps sesame oil

Clean the fish. Make diagonal cuts across the surface and rub the soy sauce over the fish. Mix the cornflour to a smooth paste with 2 tbsps water.

Heat the oil in a wok to about 190°C/375°F, then carefully add the fish. Brown the fish on both sides, then remove with a slotted spoon and drain on absorbent kitchen paper.

Remove all but 4 tbsps of the oil then reheat the wok. Add the pork, chopped garlic, chilli, spring onions, ginger, stock, salt and pickled cabbage. Stir-fry for 1-2 minutes. Return the fish to the wok and cook for a further 10 minutes. Remove the fish to a heated serving plate. Pour the cornflour mixture into the wok and cook for 1-2 minutes, until boiling and thickened. Add the sesame oil, then pour the mixture over the fish and serve.

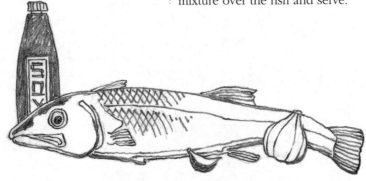

SINGAPORE FISH

Curries from Singapore and Malaysia often include fruit.
The Chinese influence on the cuisine of Singapore is obvious
– and from Singapore the Chinese learnt about curry spices
– fair exchange!

Serves 6

INGREDIENTS
460g/1lb white fish fillets
1 egg white
1 tbsp cornflour
2 tsps white wine
Salt and freshly ground black
  pepper
Oil for frying
1 large onion, cut into 1.25cm/½
  inch-thick wedges
1 tbsp mild curry powder
225g/8oz canned pineapple
  pieces, drained and juice
  reserved, or ½ a fresh
  pineapple, peeled and cubed
310g/11oz can mandarin orange
  segments, drained and juice
  reserved
1 tbsp cornflour
Juice of 1 lime
227g/8oz can sliced water
  chestnuts, drained
2 tsps sugar (optional)

Skin the fish fillets using a sharp
knife. Start at the tail end of the
fillets. Slide the knife back and
forth along the length of each
fillet, cutting the fish flesh away
from the skins. Cut the fish into
evenly-sized pieces, of about
5cm/2 inches.

Mix together the egg white,
cornflour, wine, salt and pepper.
Place the fish in the mixture and
leave to stand while heating the
oil in a large pan or wok. When
the oil is hot, fry a few pieces of
fish at a time until light golden
brown and crisp. Remove the
fish using a slotted spoon and
drain on absorbent kitchen
paper. Continue frying until all
the fish is cooked.

Remove all but 1 tbsp of the oil
from the wok and add the onion.
Stir-fry for 1-2 minutes and then
add the curry powder. Cook for a
further 1-2 minutes then add the
juices from the pineapple and
mandarin oranges and bring to
the boil.

Combine the cornflour and lime
juice into a paste and add a
spoonful of the boiling fruit juice.
Add the mixture to the wok and
cook until thickened, about 2
minutes. Taste and add sugar if
necessary. Add the fruit, water
chestnuts and fried fish to the
wok and stir until coated. Heat
through for 1 minute and serve
immediately.

STEAMED FISH WITH BLACK BEANS

*Black beans will store in an air-tight container in the
refrigerator for several weeks after opening, and may also be
frozen. To test the fish to see if it is cooked, pull back the skin
and insert the tip of a sharp knife - the fish is cooked if the
knife goes in easily.*

Serves 4

INGREDIENTS

900g/2lbs whole snapper, bass or
  bream, cleaned and scaled
2 cloves garlic, crushed
1 tbsp salted black beans
½ tsp cornflour
1 tsp sesame oil
1 tbsp light soy sauce
1 tsp sugar
1 tsp Chinese wine or 2 tsps dry
  sherry
Salt and freshly ground black
  pepper
120g/4oz canned bamboo shoots,
  cut into shreds

Wash and clean the fish and dry
with absorbent kitchen paper.
Make 3 or 4 diagonal cuts in the
flesh of the fish on each side.
Rub garlic into the cuts and place
the fish on a heat-proof dish.
Rinse the black beans in cold
water, then crush them with the
back of a spoon. Add the
cornflour, sesame oil, soy sauce,
sugar, wine, salt and pepper and
mix well. Pour the sauce over the
fish, then sprinkle the bamboo
shoots on top. Put the plate in
the top of a bamboo steamer or
on a metal trivet standing in a
wok. Add water, ensuring the
level is below the plate. Cover
and bring to the boil. Steam for
about 10 minutes, after boiling
point is reached. Ensure that the
fish is cooked, but do not
oversteam. Serve hot.

SWEET-SOUR FISH

This is an easy but impressive way of cooking a whole fish for two people – I would serve it with stir-fried vegetables. In China a river or freshwater fish would be used but a small sea bass is just as good.

Serves 2

INGREDIENTS

1 sea bass, grey mullet or carp,
  weighing about 900g/2lbs,
  cleaned and scaled
1 tbsp dry sherry
2-3 slices fresh root ginger,
  peeled
120g/4oz sugar
90ml/3 fl oz cider vinegar
1 tbsp soy sauce
2 tbsps cornflour
1 clove garlic, crushed
2 spring onions, shredded
1 small carrot, peeled and finely
  shredded
30g/1oz bamboo shoots,
  shredded

Rinse the fish well inside and out. Make three diagonal cuts on each side of the fish with a sharp knife, and trim off the fins, leaving the dorsal fin on top, and trim the tail to two neat points.

Bring enough water to the boil in a wok to just cover the fish. Gently lower the fish into the boiling water and add the sherry and ginger. Cover the wok tightly and remove it at once from the heat. Leave to stand 15-20 minutes to let the fish cook in the residual heat. To test if the fish is cooked, pull the dorsal fin – if it comes off easily the fish is done. If not, return the wok to the heat and bring to the boil. Remove from the heat and leave the fish to stand a further 5 minutes. Transfer the fish to a heated serving dish and keep it warm.

Remove all but 4 tbsps of the cooking liquid from the wok. Add the remaining ingredients including the vegetables and cook, stirring constantly, until the sauce thickens. Spoon some of the sauce over the fish to serve and hand the rest separately.

CRISPY FISH WITH CHILLI

A technique of double frying is used in this recipe to get the batter coating on the fish really crispy. The sweet, hot chilli sauce makes a perfect match for the fish.

Serves 4

INGREDIENTS
Oil for deep-frying
460g/1lb fish fillets, skinned, boned, and cut into 2.5cm/1 inch cubes

Batter
60g/2oz plain flour
Salt
1 egg, separated
1 tbsp oil
5 tbsps milk

Sauce
1 tsp grated fresh root ginger
¼ tsp chilli powder
2 tbsps tomato purée
2 tbsps tomato chutney
2 tbsps dark soy sauce
2 tbsps Chinese wine or dry sherry
2 tbsps water
1 tsp sugar
1 red chilli, seeded and finely sliced
1 clove garlic, crushed
Salt and freshly ground black pepper

Prepare the batter. Sift the flour with a pinch of salt into a bowl. Make a well in the centre, and drop in the egg yolk and oil. Mix to a smooth batter with the milk, gradually incorporating the flour. Beat well, then cover and set aside in a cool place for 30 minutes. Whisk the egg white until stiff, and fold into the batter just before using.

Heat the oil for deep-frying in a wok. Dip the fish pieces into the batter to coat them completely. When the oil is hot, carefully lower in the fish pieces and fry until cooked through and golden brown – about 10 minutes. Remove the fish with a slotted spoon. Reheat the oil and re-fry each fish piece for a further 2 minutes. Remove with a slotted spoon and drain on absorbent kitchen paper.

Carefully remove all but 1 tbsp of oil from the wok. Reheat the oil, and add all the sauce ingredients with salt and pepper to taste. Stir well over a moderate heat for 3 minutes. Increase the heat and add the fish pieces. Coat with the sauce and, when heated through, serve immediately.

STEAMED FISH IN GINGER

Steaming is an excellent method of cooking fish, keeping it moist and preserving all the delicate flavours. Smaller fish, such as red mullet, may be cooked in this way but I think that a whole large fish looks much more impressive.

Serves 4

INGREDIENTS
1.4kg/3lb whole snapper, bass or bream, cleaned and scaled
6 spring onions, cut into 5cm/2 inch lengths, then into fine shreds
3 pieces fresh root ginger, peeled and cut into fine shreds
Lemon slices and parsley to garnish

Stuffing
60g/2oz cooked rice
1 tsp grated fresh root ginger
3 spring onions, finely sliced
2 tsps light soy sauce

Prepare the stuffing. Mix together the cooked rice, grated ginger, sliced spring onion and soy sauce. Stuff the rice mixture into the cleaned fish cavity, packing it in well. Place the stuffed fish on a heat-proof plate, and arrange strips of spring onion and ginger on top. Put the plate on top of a bamboo steamer or metal trivet standing in a wok. Add water, ensuring the water level is below the plate. Cover and bring to the boil. Steam for 10 minutes from boiling point. Ensure that the fish is just cooked, but be sure not to oversteam and toughen it. Serve hot, garnished with lemon slices and parsley, if wished.

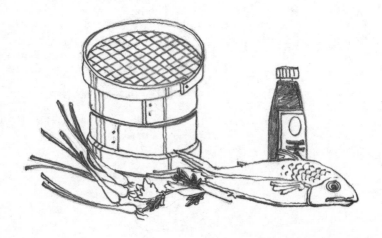

SZECHUAN FISH

*To serve Szechuan fish garnished with chilli flowers you will
need to prepare the chillies at least four hours in advance of
cooking the dish. Choose the long, thin chillies – a mixture of
red and green will look very effective.*

Serves 6

INGREDIENTS

6 red or green chillies for garnish
460g/1lb white fish fillets
Salt and freshly ground black
  pepper
1 egg
75g/2½ oz flour
90ml/3 fl oz white wine
Oil for frying
60g/2oz cooked ham, cut into
  small dice
2.5cm/1 inch piece fresh ginger,
  finely diced
½-1 red or green chilli, peeled
  and seeded and finely diced
6 water chestnuts, finely diced
4 spring onions, finely chopped
3 tbsps light soy sauce
1 tsp cider vinegar or rice wine
  vinegar
½ tsp ground Szechuan pepper
  (optional)
280ml/½ pint fish or vegetable
  stock
1 tbsp cornflour mixed with 2
  tbsps water
2 tsps sugar

To prepare the garnish, choose
unblemished chillies with stems
on. Using a small, sharp knife,
cut the chillies into strips, starting
from the pointed end. Cut down
to within 1.25cm/½ inch of the
stem end. Rinse out the seeds
under cold running water and
place the chillies in iced water.
Leave to soak for at least 4 hours
or overnight until they open up.

Cut the fish fillets into 5cm/2
inch pieces and season with salt
and pepper. Beat the egg well
and add the flour and wine to
make a batter. Dredge the fish
lightly with extra flour and then
dip it into the batter. Coat the
fish well. Heat a wok and, when
hot, add enough oil to deep-fry
the fish. When the oil is hot, fry a
few pieces of fish at a time, until
golden brown. Drain the fish
pieces on absorbent kitchen
paper and repeat until all the fish
is cooked.

Remove all but 1 tbsp of oil from
the wok and add the ham,
ginger, diced chilli, water
chestnuts and spring onions.
Cook for about 1 minute then
add the soy sauce and vinegar. If
using Szechuan pepper, add it
now. Stir well and cook for a
further 1 minute. Remove the
vegetables from the pan and set
them aside. Pour the stock into
the wok and bring to the boil.
When boiling, add 1 spoonful of
the hot stock to the cornflour
mixture, then add the mixture to
the stock and reboil, stirring
constantly until thickened. Stir in
the sugar and return the fish and
vegetables to the sauce. Heat
through for 30 seconds and serve
immediately.

BAKED TROUT WITH BLACK BEAN SAUCE

This is a very robust way of cooking trout – and it is very delicious! Any whole fish could be cooked in this way. Have the various sets of mixtures prepared before you start the fish.

Serves 4

INGREDIENTS

680g/1½lb trout (cleaned with head on)
1 tsp salt
½ tsp pepper
½ tsp ground ginger
2 tbsps shredded spring onions
1 tbsp shredded fresh root ginger
2 tbsps vegetable oil
1 tbsp black bean sauce
1 tsp dried red chilli, chopped
½ tsp sugar
1 tbsp light soy sauce
1 tbsp pale dry sherry
1 tbsp shredded spring onion
2 tsps shredded fresh root ginger
2 tsps shredded red chilli
1 tbsp light soy sauce
1 tsp sesame oil

Preheat the oven to 200°C/400°F/Gas Mark 6. Lightly score the fish by making diagonal cuts at 2.5cm/1 inch intervals on both sides of the body. Mix together the salt, pepper and ground ginger and rub this mixture over the inside and outside of the fish. Lay the fish in a heatproof pan, casserole or gratin dish. Scatter the shredded spring onions and root ginger over the fish. Heat the vegetable oil in a small pan until almost smoking and pour over the fish. Mix together the black bean sauce, dried chilli, sugar, light soy sauce and sherry. Spoon the mixture over the fish and cover the dish tightly with foil. Cook for 15-20 minutes in the preheated oven.

Mix together the 1 tbsp shredded spring onion, ½ tbsp shredded root ginger and ¼ tbsp shredded red chilli. When the fish is cooked, pile the shredded vegetables on top of the fish and drizzle with the soy sauce and sesame oil before serving.

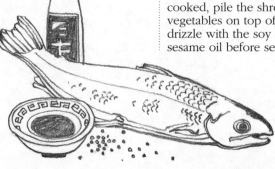
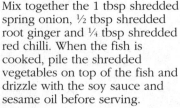

TROUT FILLETS WITH GINGER & SPRING ONION

Sea trout are larger than river trout; use either fish for this recipe. The sauce is slightly sweet and finishes the dish perfectly.

Serves 4

INGREDIENTS
4 sea trout fillets
Salt and freshly ground black
  pepper
1 spring onion, chopped
1 tsp chopped fresh root ginger
120ml/4 fl oz white wine vinegar
120ml/4 fl oz soy sauce
3 tsps sugar
120ml/4 fl oz fish stock

Season the trout fillets with salt and pepper. Lay them in a steamer basket and scatter the spring onion and ginger over. Set to one side. Mix together the vinegar, soy sauce, sugar and fish stock in a saucepan. Heat until boiling and allow to reduce and thicken. Steam the trout for about 5 minutes while the sauce is cooking, then serve the fillets with the sauce spooned over.

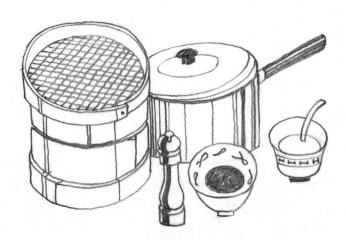

BREAM WITH PINEAPPLE

Pineapple is widely used in Oriental cookery – it has a sweet freshness which helps to bring out the flavour of other ingredients, and it complements fish particularly well.

Serves 4

INGREDIENTS

1 large sea bream
2 tbsps oil
1-2 cloves garlic, finely chopped
4 slices of canned pineapple, cut into small pieces
1 tbsp soy sauce
60ml/2 fl oz pineapple syrup, from the can
280ml/½ pint fish stock
1 tsp cornflour, combined with a little water
Salt and freshly ground black pepper

Cut the fins off the fish, and remove the fillets with a sharp knife. Skin the fillets and cut into bite-sized pieces. Discard the head, tail and bones or save them for stock.

Heat 1 tbsp of the oil in a wok and stir-fry the garlic and the pineapple pieces. Pour off any excess oil and add the soy sauce, pineapple syrup and fish stock. Allow the sauce to reduce a little and then add the cornflour paste, stirring continuously until the sauce boils and thickens. Remove the sauce from the wok and keep warm. Heat the remaining oil in the cleaned wok and stir-fry the pieces of fish, seasoning them with salt and pepper. Shake the wok frequently to cook the fish evenly. Serve the bream with the sauce spooned over the fish.

WHITING FRITTERS WITH COLD FISH SAUCE

Whiting is a very under-rated fish. It is relatively inexpensive to buy and has a good flavour and texture. You will need to fry the fish in several batches to prevent the pieces from sticking together, so keep the cooked whiting hot in a warming oven until cooking is complete.

Serves 4

INGREDIENTS
175g/6oz plain flour, sieved
1 tsp baking powder
120ml/4 fl oz water
1 egg, beaten
1 tsp oil
460g/1lb whiting fillets
Salt and freshly ground black
  pepper
Oil for deep-frying

Sauce
1 tbsp fish sauce
1 tbsp soy sauce
1 tbsp fish stock
1 tsp freshly chopped mint

Make a batter by mixing the sieved flour and the baking powder together in a bowl, then mix in the water, followed by the egg. Add the oil and a good pinch of salt and beat all the ingredients together well. Set the batter aside to rest for a few minutes.

Season the whiting fillets with salt and pepper and cut them into thin strips. Heat the oil for deep-frying. Dip the whiting strips into the batter and fry them in the hot oil until crisp and golden. Remove the fritters with a slotted spoon and drain them on absorbent kitchen paper. Keep hot.

Meanwhile, mix together the sauce ingredients and serve the sauce with the hot whiting fritters.

MONKFISH WITH ONIONS & VINEGAR SAUCE

Monkfish is a firm-fleshed white fish which keeps its shape well during cooking. The onion and vinegar sauce is slightly sharp and very Oriental.

Serves 4

INGREDIENTS

900g/2lb monkfish tail, cleaned
2 tbsps oil
2 large onions, finely sliced
2 tbsps white wine vinegar
2 tsps sugar
1 tbsp soy sauce
340ml/12 fl oz fish stock
½ tsp chopped fresh root ginger
Salt and freshly ground black
  pepper
1 tbsp cornflour

Prepare the fish by pulling off the skin. Fillet the fish by sliding a sharp knife between the flesh and the central bones on each side. Cut both fillets in half.

Heat the oil in a wok, add the onions and stir-fry gently until soft, then ease them up the sides of the wok. Add the fish fillets to the wok, stir-fry for 1 minute, then push the onions back into the wok with the fish. Add the vinegar to the pan and boil until almost evaporated, then stir in the sugar, soy sauce, fish stock and ginger. Season with salt and pepper to taste, stir well, cover and cook gently for 7-8 minutes. Remove the fish from the wok, cut into thin slices and keep warm on a hot plate or in a warm oven. Mix the cornflour to a paste with a little cold water, add to the sauce and stir continuously until boiling and thickened. Place the onions and their sauce on a hot serving plate. Place the sliced fish on top and serve immediately.

SEA BASS IN FIVE-SPICE SAUCE

This delicious sauce is wonderful with fish but is also excellent with pork, which may then be barbecued – I use it to marinate pork tenderloin.

Serves 4

INGREDIENTS
460g/1lb sea bass fillets
1 tbsp fish sauce
1 tbsp Chinese wine
1 tsp oyster sauce
½ tsp finely chopped fresh root ginger
2 shallots, chopped
2 tsps five-spice powder
Salt and freshly ground black pepper
1 tbsp oil

Cut the sea bass fillets into thin slices and arrange the slices on a plate. Combine the fish sauce, wine, oyster sauce, chopped ginger, shallots and five-spice powder and pour over the fish. Season the fish with salt and pepper and leave to marinate in the sauce mixture for 1 hour.

Heat the oil in a frying pan; drain the fish slices and fry briefly for 30 seconds on each side. Serve immediately. The sauce may be heated and served with the fish.

BREAM IN SWEET &
SOUR SAUCE

Bream is a lovely fish with a delicious flavour. Don't be afraid that the sweet and sour sauce will mask the flavour of the fish - they complement each other well.

Serves 4

INGREDIENTS
1 sea bream, weighing about
   800g/1¾ lbs
½ red pepper, seeded
½ green pepper, seeded
¼ cucumber
1 tbsp oil
1 tsp finely chopped fresh root
   ginger
2 cloves garlic, finely chopped
2 spring onions, finely chopped
¼ small fresh green chilli, seeded
3 tbsps pineapple juice
2 tbsps crushed tomato or
   passata
150ml/¼ pint fish stock
1 tsp cornflour, combined with a
   little water
1 tbsp vinegar
Salt and freshly ground black
   pepper
1 sheet dried seaweed (optional)
1 tbsp freshly chopped chives to
   garnish

Scale and clean the bream then fillet the fish, removing any bones, and cut into medium-sized pieces. Cut the red and green peppers and the cucumber into fine julienne strips.

Heat the oil in a wok and cook the vegetables, ginger, garlic, spring onion and the chilli for 1 minute. Add the pineapple juice, the crushed tomato or passata and the fish stock. Simmer over a low heat for 2 minutes. Thicken the sauce with the cornflour paste, stirring continuously, until boiling. Remove and discard the chilli, add the vinegar and season with salt and pepper to taste.

Steam the bream over water containing strips of the dried seaweed, if using. Serve the fish accompanied by the sweet and sour sauce and sprinkled with the chopped chives.

CHINESE RAW FISH

Don't decide that raw fish is not to your taste before you have tried it! The secret is to slice the fish very thinly and to allow at least 30 minutes for the fish to marinate.

Serves 4

INGREDIENTS

225g/8oz firm-fleshed fish fillets, e.g. haddock or cod
225g/8oz sea bass
1 tsp finely chopped fresh root ginger
1-2 cloves garlic, finely chopped
1 tsp finely chopped shallot
Juice of 1 lemon
10 coriander seeds, crushed
Few drops sesame oil
Salt and freshly ground black pepper
1 tbsp freshly chopped chives to garnish

Slice the fish very thinly, spread the slices out on a plate and sprinkle with the chopped ginger, garlic and shallot. Drizzle with the lemon juice and sprinkle with the crushed coriander seeds, then finally add the sesame oil. Allow to marinate for 30 minutes. Season with salt and pepper to taste, garnish with the chopped chives and serve.

TROUT IN OYSTER SAUCE

This is a most unusual way to serve trout but is quite delicious! The orange juice is a wonderful flavouring.

Serves 4

INGREDIENTS
2 trout
Salt and freshly ground black pepper
2 tbsps oyster sauce
120g/4oz bamboo shoots, cut in matchsticks
1 tbsp oil
1 tsp finely chopped fresh root ginger
1-2 cloves garlic, finely chopped
½ green pepper, seeded and finely chopped
½ red pepper, seeded and finely chopped
½ onion, finely chopped
1 tsp sugar
1 tsp white wine vinegar
Juice of ½ orange
2 tbsps soy sauce
225ml/8 fl oz fish stock
1 tsp cornflour, combined with a little water

Fillet the trout, then cut the fillets into several pieces. Season with salt and pepper, and brush each one with oyster sauce, then stack in pairs and set aside. Blanch the bamboo shoots, then rinse and allow them to drain.

Heat the oil in a wok and stir-fry the ginger, garlic, peppers, onion and bamboo shoots for 2-3 minutes. Add the sugar, vinegar, orange juice, soy sauce and fish stock and cook for 3 minutes. Season to taste, then add the cornflour, stirring continuously until boiling and thickened. Steam the trout pieces separately for approximately 3 minutes, or until just cooked. Serve the fish on a bed of the vegetables in sauce.

STEAMED SEA BASS

Shred the root ginger and spring onion garnish for this steamed bass very finely for maximum flavour. If the fish is too large to lay across a plate in your steamer, curl it round on its belly.

Serves 4

INGREDIENTS
1 whole sea bass (weighing
  about 680g/1½lbs)
2 spring onions
2 slices fresh root ginger, peeled
  and chopped
1-2 rashers bacon

Sauce and garnish
3-4 slices fresh root ginger
2 spring onions
1½ tbsps soy sauce
1 tbsp pale dry sherry
1½ tbsps oil

Clean and gut the fish. Cut the spring onions into 5cm/2 inch pieces and chop the bacon finely.

Prepare the sauce and garnish. Cut the ginger and spring onions into fine shreds. Mix together the soy sauce and sherry. Place the bass on a heatproof dish that will fit in your steamer and scatter the chopped spring onion and ginger and the bacon over the fish. Place the dish in the steamer, cover and steam vigorously for 15-20 minutes. Remove the chopped vegetables and bacon from the fish.

Pour the sherry and soy mixture over the fish just before serving and garnish with the shredded ginger and spring onions. Heat the oil until almost smoking and pour over the fish, creating a loud sizzle. Serve immediately.

KUNG PAO PRAWNS WITH CASHEW NUTS

*I love cashew nuts with prawns, with chicken, on their own –
any way! Perhaps Kung Pao felt the same way, but no-one
seems to know who the creator of this recipe actually was!*

Serves 6

INGREDIENTS
½ tsp chopped fresh root ginger
1 tsp chopped garlic
1½ tbsps cornflour
¼ tsp bicarbonate of soda
Salt and freshly ground black
 pepper
¼ tsp sugar
460g/1lb uncooked prawns
4 tbsps oil
1 small onion, chopped
1 large or 2 small courgettes, cut
 into 1.25cm/½ inch cubes
1 small red pepper, cut into
 1.25cm/½ inch cubes
60g/2oz cashew nuts

Sauce
175ml/6fl oz chicken stock
1 tbsp cornflour
2 tsps chilli sauce
2 tsps bean paste (optional)
2 tsps sesame oil
1 tbsp dry sherry or rice wine

Mix together the ginger, garlic,
cornflour, bicarbonate of soda,
salt, pepper and sugar. If the
prawns are unpeeled, remove the
shells and the dark vein running
along the rounded side. Cut any
large prawns into 2. Add the
prawns to the dry ingredients
and leave to stand for 20
minutes.

Heat the oil in a wok and, when
hot, add the prawns and
flavourings. Cook, stirring over
high heat, for about 20 seconds,
or just until the prawns change
colour. Transfer to a plate using a
slotted spoon. Add the onion to
the same oil in the wok and
cook for about 1 minute, then
add the courgettes and red
pepper and cook for about 30
seconds. Mix the sauce
ingredients together and add
them to the wok. Cook, stirring
constantly, until the sauce is
slightly thickened. Return the
prawns to the wok with the
cashew nuts and cook until
heated through completely.

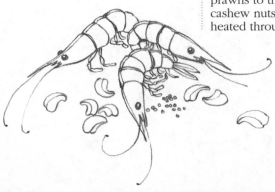

CRAB WITH BAMBOO SHOOTS

I live very close to Selsey so I find it easy to get fresh crabs in season. Canned crabmeat is a good alternative – I find that the meat canned in the Far East has the best flavour.

Serves 4

INGREDIENTS
1 green or red chilli
225-280g/8-10oz crabmeat
225g/8oz bamboo shoots
1 tbsp oil
4 slices fresh root ginger, peeled
½ onion, chopped
1 tsp vinegar
1 tsp sugar
225ml/8 fl oz fish stock
1 tsp cornflour, blended with a
    little water
Salt and freshly ground black
    pepper
1 tbsp freshly chopped chives

Prepare the chilli. Cut off the stalk end, slice the chilli in half and remove the pith and seeds from the centre. Chop the chilli as finely as possible. Pick over the crabmeat and remove any shell. Cut the bamboo shoots into thin slices and blanch them in boiling, lightly salted water for 2 minutes, then drain.

Heat the oil in a wok and stir-fry the ginger, onion and bamboo shoots for 1 minute. Stir in the crab and as much of the chilli as you like, and fry for a further 1 minute. Stir in the vinegar, sugar and fish stock and cook for 5 minutes over a gentle heat. Thicken by adding the cornflour paste, stirring continuously until boiling. Season to taste with salt and pepper, garnish with chopped chives and serve.

SEAFOOD COMBINATION

Using prawns, white fish fillets and squid for this seafood combination gives an excellent variety of fishy textures to the dish. Cod, haddock, plaice or any white fish is suitable.

Serves 4

INGREDIENTS
1 tbsp dry white wine
½ tsp salt
1 egg white
1 tsp grated fresh root ginger
1 tsp cornflour
225g/8oz prawns or shrimps, shelled and de-veined
120g/4oz white fish fillets, cut into 2.5cm/1 inch cubes
120g/4oz mangetout
120g/4oz squid tubes, cut into 2.5cm/1 inch rings
Oil for deep-frying
1 carrot, cut into matchsticks
1 stick celery, sliced diagonally

Combine the wine, salt, egg white, grated ginger and cornflour in a bowl and mix well. Add the prawns and fish, coat evenly and thoroughly, then drain, reserving the sauce. Blanch the mangetout in boiling water for 1 minute and drain. Open up the squid rings and score each one with a sharp knife into a lattice pattern.

Heat the oil in a wok. Deep-fry the prawns, fish and squid for 2 minutes. Remove from the wok using a slotted spoon and drain on absorbent kitchen paper. Carefully pour off all but 1 tbsp of oil from the wok. Heat the oil again and stir-fry the carrot and celery for 3 minutes. Add the mangetout and stir-fry for a further 3 minutes. Add any remaining sauce and stir. Add the seafood and toss well until heated through. Serve immediately.

QUICK FRIED PRAWNS

This is so quick and easy to prepare and requires next-to-no cooking. Use cooked or raw prawns, adjusting the brief cooking period accordingly.

Serves 4-6

INGREDIENTS
900g/2lbs cooked prawns in their shells
2 cloves garlic, crushed
2.5cm/1 inch piece fresh root ginger, peeled and finely chopped
1 tbsp freshly chopped coriander
3 tbsps oil
1 tbsp rice wine or dry sherry
1½ tbsps light soy sauce
Chopped spring onions to garnish

Shell the prawns except for the tail ends – this gives a most attractive presentation. Place the prawns in a bowl with the remaining ingredients, except for the garnish, and leave to marinate for 30 minutes. Heat a wok and add the prawns and their marinade. Stir-fry briefly to heat the prawns, taking care not to overcook them. Scatter the chopped onions over the prawns and serve.

SQUID WITH BROCCOLI & CAULIFLOWER

I adore squid – fried, steamed, stewed in it's own ink, any way at all! I was always intrigued as to how the Chinese got it to such a different shape to everyone else – well, once I started Chinese cooking, I soon found out!

Serves 4

INGREDIENTS
460g/1lb squid tubes
150ml/¼ pint oil for deep-frying
1 onion, roughly chopped
2 sticks celery, sliced diagonally
225g/8oz broccoli florets
225g/8oz cauliflower florets
½ tsp grated fresh root ginger
1 tbsp cornflour
2 tbsps water
2 tbsps light soy sauce
2 tbsps Chinese wine or dry
    sherry
2 tbsps oyster sauce
½ tsp sesame oil
½ tsp sugar
Salt and freshly ground black
    pepper

Cut cleaned squid lengthways down the centre. Flatten out with the inside uppermost. With a sharp knife make a lattice design, cutting deep into the squid flesh. This tenderises the squid and makes it curl during cooking.

Heat the oil in a wok. Add the squid and cook until it curls, then remove it from the wok with a slotted spoon and drain on absorbent kitchen paper. Carefully pour off all but 1 tbsp of oil from the wok. Add the onion, celery, broccoli, cauliflower and ginger, and stir-fry for 3 minutes. Mix the cornflour to a paste with the water, and add the soy sauce, wine, oyster sauce, sesame oil, sugar, and salt and pepper. Mix well and add to the wok. Bring to the boil and simmer for 3 minutes, stirring continuously. Return the squid to the wok and cook until heated through. Place in a warm serving dish and serve hot with rice.

SCRAMBLED EGGS WITH CRABMEAT

I have often eaten scrambled eggs laced with a few smoked salmon trimmings, which is delicious. With crabmeat it is even more special.

Serves 4

INGREDIENTS
3 Chinese dried mushrooms, soaked for 15 minutes in warm water
8 eggs, beaten
Few drops sesame oil
1 tsp rice wine
1 tbsp soy sauce
175g/6oz crabmeat
Salt and freshly ground black pepper

Cook the mushrooms in boiling, salted water for 15 minutes. Rinse in fresh water and set aside to drain then slice.

In a large bowl mix together the eggs, sliced mushrooms, sesame oil, rice wine, soy sauce and the crabmeat. Season with salt and pepper. Cook by stirring the eggs over a very gentle heat in a nonstick frying pan.. The eggs will thicken slowly. Serve when cooked to your liking.

PRAWNS & GINGER

I love the flavour of fresh ginger – it is fresh, dramatic and excitingly different. It marries particularly well with shellfish.

Serves 6

INGREDIENTS
2 tbsps oil
680g/1½lbs peeled prawns
2.5cm/1 inch piece fresh root
  ginger, peeled and finely
  chopped
2 cloves of garlic, finely chopped
2-3 spring onions, chopped
1 leek, white part only, cut into
  strips
120g/4oz peas, shelled
175g/6oz bean sprouts
2 tbsps dark soy sauce
1 tsp sugar
Pinch of salt

Heat the oil in a wok and stir-fry the prawns for 2-3 minutes. Remove the prawns with a slotted spoon and set aside. Reheat the oil and add the ginger and garlic. Stir quickly, then add the onions, leek and peas. Stir-fry for 2-3 minutes. Add the bean sprouts and prawns to the cooked vegetables. Stir in the soy sauce, sugar and salt and cook for 2 minutes. Serve immediately.

BROCCOLI WITH OYSTERS

This recipe has a touch of luxury about it and is suitable as part of a meal for a special occasion. Use an old, but sharp, knife to open the oysters – they can be very reluctant!

Serves 4

INGREDIENTS
680g/1½lbs broccoli
8 large oysters
280ml/½ pint fish stock
1 tsp chopped fresh root ginger
1 sprig fresh thyme
1 tbsp oyster sauce
1 tsp cornflour, combined with a
   little water
Salt and freshly ground black
   pepper

Choose fresh, green broccoli. Cut off the tough stalks, trim and rinse well. Cook the broccoli in boiling, lightly salted water, until tender but still crisp. Refresh by plunging into cold water and set aside to drain.

Open the oyster shells, cut out and set aside the oysters, and discard both juice and shell. Heat the fish stock and add the ginger, thyme and broccoli. Cook, covered, for 5 minutes. Remove the broccoli with a slotted spoon and add the oysters. Poach them for 1 minute, then remove with a slotted spoon and place on a hot serving dish. Stir the oyster sauce into the fish stock, remove the thyme and stir in the cornflour paste. Cook until boiling and thickened, then adjust the seasoning as necessary. Serve the oysters surrounded by the broccoli and accompanied by the sauce.

PRAWNS WITH VEGETABLES

A quick dish which will serve four as part of a Chinese meal, or one or two as a supper dish.

Serves 4

INGREDIENTS
½ cucumber
225g/8oz bean sprouts
8 Chinese dried black
   mushrooms, soaked in warm
   water for 15 minutes
2 tbsps peanut oil
1 clove garlic, chopped
1 tsp sugar
1 tsp oyster sauce
1 tsp white wine vinegar
Salt and freshly ground black
   pepper
1 tsp oil
20 prawns, peeled and deveined
2 tbsps cornflour
1 tbsp soy sauce
1 tbsp sesame oil

Peel the cucumber and cut into fine julienne strips. Rinse and drain the bean sprouts. Drain the mushrooms and cook in boiling, salted water for 15 minutes. Rinse and set aside to drain again.

Heat the peanut oil in a wok and stir-fry the garlic, bean sprouts and mushrooms for 1 minute. Add the cucumber, sugar, oyster sauce, vinegar, salt and pepper, and cook for 2 minutes, stirring continuously. Heat the remaining oil in a frying pan. Toss the prawns in the cornflour and fry until cooked. Transfer the vegetables to a serving platter. Top with the fried prawns. Sprinkle with soy sauce and sesame oil and serve immediately.

SWEET & SOUR SHELLFISH

This recipe uses clams but, as the name suggests, any shellfish could be cooked in this way. Mussels, prawns, squid rings – you choose! Do try not to overcook the shellfish – they easily become tough.

Serves 4

INGREDIENTS

20 clams, rinsed in plenty of running water
150ml/¼ pint Chinese wine
1 tbsp oil
1 tsp finely chopped fresh root ginger
1-2 cloves garlic, finely chopped
½ red pepper, seeded and cut into thin matchsticks
½ green pepper, seeded and cut into thin matchsticks
¼ cucumber, peeled and cut into thin matchsticks
1 tbsp soy sauce
2 tbsps pineapple or orange juice
1 tsp white wine vinegar
Salt and freshly ground black pepper

Place the clams in a large saucepan, pour in the wine, cover, and place over a high heat to open the shells, which should take approximately 3-5 minutes. Remove the pan from the heat and the clams from their shells. Drain the cooking liquid through a very fine sieve and reserve. Keep the shells to one side.

Heat the oil in a wok and stir-fry the ginger, garlic, vegetables and clams for 2 minutes, then stir in the soy sauce, 4 tbsps of the reserved cooking liquid, the pineapple or orange juice, and the vinegar. Season with salt and pepper to taste. Cook until the sauce is slightly reduced and the clams are tender. Replace the cooked clams, with the sauce, in the reserved shells. Warm through in a hot oven for 2 minutes if necessary and serve immediately.

BREADED PRAWNS WITH FRESH TOMATO SALAD

Combining fried prawns with a fresh tomato salad is fresh, simple and memorable. Always skin tomatoes from the flower end – it's much easier that way!

Serves 4

INGREDIENTS
5 ripe tomatoes
1 tsp finely chopped fresh root
  ginger
1 tbsp freshly chopped chives
Salt and freshly ground black
  pepper
24 fresh prawns
2 tbsps oil
2 tbsps plain flour
2 eggs, beaten
4 tbsps fresh breadcrumbs

Plunge the tomatoes into a bowl of boiling water for 15 seconds. Rinse immediately in cold water and allow to cool. Skin, seed and finely chop the tomatoes. Mix the ginger and chives with the tomatoes, season and allow to marinate for 2 hours in the refrigerator. Shell the prawns, leaving the tails.

Heat the oil in a frying pan or wok. Dredge the prawns in the flour, then dip them in the beaten egg, and finally coat them in the breadcrumbs. Fry until golden in the hot oil. Serve the fried prawns on a bed of chilled tomato salad, garnished with chopped chives, if wished.

TRIPLE FRY OF 'THREE SEA FLAVOURS'

I normally advise against using frozen scallops as they collapse when defrosted. However, as the three types of shellfish in this recipe are finely chopped, frozen scallops are fine.

Serves 3-4

INGREDIENTS

120g/4oz large peeled prawns
4 scallops
120g/4oz squid tubes
4 tsps salted black beans
2 slices fresh root ginger, peeled
2 spring onions
2 cloves garlic
1 small red pepper, seeded
6 tbsps oil
120ml/4 fl oz chicken stock
1 tbsp soy sauce
1 tbsp chilli sauce
1 tbsp cornflour blended with 3 tsps water
1½ tsps sesame oil
1 tbsp sherry
Salt and freshly ground black pepper

Finely chop the prawns, scallops and squid. Soak the black beans in warm water for 5 minutes, then drain and chop them finely. Shred the root ginger, cut the spring onion into 2.5cm/1 inch pieces and chop the garlic. Cut the red pepper into 2.5cm/1 inch pieces.

Heat 4 tbsps of oil in a large frying pan or wok, add the chopped seafood and stir-fry quickly for 1-2 minutes. Remove the seafood with a slotted spoon and drain on absorbent kitchen paper. Add the remaining oil, heat and add the ginger, garlic and black beans. Stir-fry for 1 minute then add the spring onions and pepper with the stock and cook for 1 minute. Add the soy and chilli sauces and return the seafood to the wok, stirring to mix. Finally add the cornflour paste, the sesame oil and sherry. Bring rapidly to the boil, stirring continuously, season to taste then serve.

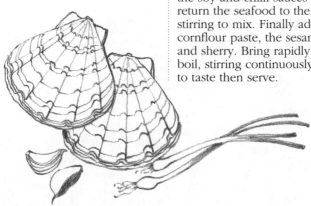

STEAMED PRAWNS

Don't throw the courgette peel away – it is an integral part of this dish! The peel is wrapped around the prawns giving a most attractive pink and green presentation. Use the courgette flesh in a vegetable stir-fry to serve with the prawns.

Serves 4

INGREDIENTS
1 tbsp fish sauce
1 tbsp water
1 tbsp wine vinegar
1 tbsp soy sauce
2 tsps sugar
10 freshly chopped mint leaves
1 shallot, chopped
Salt and freshly ground black pepper
12 fresh prawns, peeled and cleaned
2 medium-sized courgettes, peeled and the peel cut into long strips

Mix together the fish sauce, water, vinegar, soy sauce, sugar, mint, shallot, salt and pepper. Stir well and set aside for at least 1 hour. Just before serving time, season the prawns with plenty of salt and pepper, then roll the strips of courgette peel around the prawns and cook them in a Chinese steamer for 5 minutes. Serve the prawns piping hot, accompanied by the sauce.

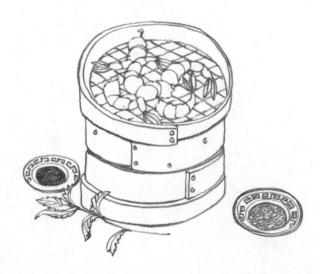

GINGER SCALLOPS IN OYSTER SAUCE

Take great care not to overcook the scallops as they will become tough and rubbery. Frozen scallops should only be used in an emergency – they almost disintegrate when defrosted.

Serves 4

INGREDIENTS
460g/1lb scallops, cleaned, dried on absorbent kitchen paper, and sliced
Salt
2 tbsps vegetable oil
2.5cm/1 inch fresh root ginger, peeled and very thinly sliced
10 spring onions, sliced diagonally into 2.5cm/1 inch slices
5 tbsps light stock, or 5 tbsps hot water and half a chicken stock cube

Sauce
1 tbsp oyster sauce
1 tbsp light soy sauce
½ tsp sesame oil
1 tsp cornflour
Pinch of sugar
1 tsp grated fresh root ginger

Prepare the sauce: combine the oyster sauce, soy sauce, sesame oil, cornflour, sugar and grated ginger in a bowl and set aside. Sprinkle the scallops with a pinch of salt. Heat a wok and add the oil. Add the sliced ginger and spring onions and stir-fry gently for 1 minute, then raise the heat to high. Add the scallops and stir-fry for 1 minute, then stir in the sauce mixture. Remove the wok from the heat and gradually add the stock. Return to the heat and bring to the boil, stirring continuously. Simmer gently for 3 minutes, until the sauce is slightly thickened. Adjust the seasoning, then serve immediately with boiled rice.

CHINESE LEAVES WITH OYSTERS

Are oysters a flavour or a funny sensation? Eaten raw they may be the latter, but cooked in this way with vegetables they are wonderful.

Serves 4

INGREDIENTS
12 large oysters
460g/1lb Chinese leaves
1 tbsp oil
225g/8oz bacon, diced
4 tbsps fish stock
Salt and freshly ground black
  pepper

Use large oysters if possible. If you have to use the smaller variety, increase the number accordingly. Open the oysters, taking care to protect your hand by wrapping a tea-towel around the oysters – the shells are sharp! Cut the oysters away from the shell, reserving the juice. Shred the Chinese leaves.

Heat the oil in a wok and stir-fry the bacon. Stir the Chinese leaves into the wok and add the fish stock. Check the seasoning, adding salt and pepper to taste, and continue cooking until the Chinese leaves are to your liking. Place the oysters and their juice on top of the Chinese leaves and poach for approximately 2 minutes. Remove the oysters and place on a hot serving plate. Serve immediately, with the cooked Chinese leaves.

HONEY SESAME PRAWNS

These delicious prawns make a splendid fish course with just a little salad garnish and lots of fresh lemon to squeeze over them. You could drizzle a little hot chilli sauce over them for variety.

Serves 4

INGREDIENTS

120g/4oz self-raising flour
Salt and freshly ground black pepper
1 egg, lightly beaten
150ml/¼ pint water
460g/1lb prawns or shrimps, shelled and de-veined
2 tbsps cornflour
Oil for deep-frying
1 tbsp sesame oil
2 tbsps honey
1 tbsp sesame seeds

Sift the flour, salt and pepper into a bowl. Make a well in the centre and add the egg and water. Mix well, gradually bringing in the flour. Beat to a smooth batter and set aside for 10 minutes. Meanwhile, toss the prawns in the cornflour to coat well. Shake off any excess cornflour.
Carefully stir the prawns into the batter and coat them thoroughly.

Heat the oil in a wok and add the prawns, a few at a time. Cook until the batter is golden, then remove the prawns with a slotted spoon, drain on absorbent kitchen paper and keep warm. Repeat until all the prawns have been fried.

Carefully pour the hot oil from the wok. Add the sesame oil and heat gently, then add the honey and stir until well mixed and heated through. Add the prawns to the mixture and toss well. Sprinkle with sesame seeds and toss again. Serve immediately.

SCALLOPS WITH ASPARAGUS

In any cuisine the combination of scallops and asparagus means summer! Two tastes that epitomise sunshine and lazy days – this recipe is ideal for such occasions as it is so quick to prepare.

Serves 4

INGREDIENTS
16 scallops
16 green asparagus spears
1 tbsp oil

Dipping Sauce
1 tbsp soy sauce
2 tsps sugar
½ spring onion, finely chopped
1 tbsp oil
1 tsp wine vinegar
Salt and freshly ground black
  pepper

Prise open the scallops with the point of a sharp knife and extract the scallop and the coral. Rinse well and allow to dry on a clean tea-towel. Boil the asparagus in salted water until tender, and refresh in cold water. Drain and cut in half lengthways, if the spears are large.

Make the dipping sauce by combining the soy sauce, sugar, spring onion, oil, vinegar and salt and pepper to taste. Brush the scallops and corals with oil and season them with salt and pepper. Preheat a grill or oil a frying pan, and quickly grill or sauté the scallops, turning them carefully. Cook for 1 minute on each side. Serve the scallops with the asparagus to dip in the sauce.

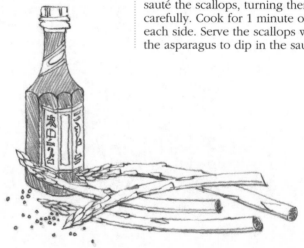

STIR-FRIED PRAWNS &
MANGETOUT

*Prawns and mangetout both have delicate flavours and
occasionally it is good to let them shine through without
strong spices to mask them. I like to serve this with
thread egg noodles.*

Serves 4

INGREDIENTS
120g/4oz mangetout, trimmed
4 tbsps peanut oil
225g/8oz prawns or shrimps,
  shelled and de-veined
2 tbsps dry white wine
Juice of half a lemon
1 tbsp light soy sauce
Salt and freshly ground black
  pepper
Parsley to garnish

Blanch the mangetout in boiling
salted water for 1 minute, then
drain and set aside. Heat a wok,
add the peanut oil, and stir-fry
the prawns for 30 seconds. Add
the mangetout, dry white wine,
lemon juice, soy sauce, and a
little salt and pepper, and toss
together until heated through.
Season to taste and garnish with
parsley. Serve immediately with
boiled rice.

STIR-FRIED LOBSTER WITH GINGER

I have to confess that lobster often manages not to impress me, especially when served cold. Served hot and flavoured with ginger it is quite delicious.

Serves 4

INGREDIENTS

2 cooked lobsters, each weighing 340g/12oz
1 courgette
1 tbsp oil
2 tsps chopped fresh root ginger
1 tbsp oyster sauce
120ml/4 fl oz fish stock
Salt and freshly ground black pepper
1 tsp cornflour, combined with a little water

Shell the lobsters and remove the meat, or ask your fishmonger to do this for you. Slice the lobster meat into bite-sized pieces. Slice the courgette thinly.

Heat the oil in a wok and stir-fry the ginger. Add the courgette and cook until tender but still crisp, then add the lobster and heat through. Pour in the oyster sauce and the fish stock, season with salt and pepper to taste and allow the sauce to reduce and thicken slightly. Add the cornflour paste and cook, stirring continuously, until thickened. Serve immediately.

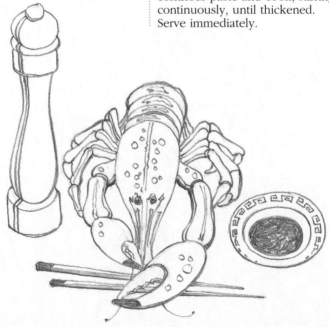

CHICKEN & DUCK

Chicken and duck are the most widely eaten poultry in China, although pigeon and quail are also popular and some geese are prepared for the table. It is impossible to know even a little about Chinese food without the realisation that crispy duck and chicken are amongst the most popular dishes in the Chinese repertoire.

A Good Mixer
Chicken is the most highly prized, as well as the most widely used, of all poultry in China. It is eaten daily in the homes of the affluent but they seldom tire of it as it is so versatile and can be prepared in quite literally hundreds of ways. Chicken has

quite a light, mild flavour and therefore absorbs seasonings readily, making it a good mixer with so many different vegetables. It also blends well with prawns and other shellfish in dishes such as fried rice and mixed chop suey.

What, No Oven?

It seems surprising but, even now, most homes in China do not have an oven – you will find that very few recipes in this book call for an oven and that virtually all the food is cooked by stir-frying, steaming, dry frying or braising (that is, braising in a pan rather than in the oven). It is therefore very unusual to find a recipe for chicken which requires roasting; to achieve such a result one would have to make friends with the local restaurateur who might have an oven.

Pluck Your Own

The love of fine cuisine is deeply rooted in the Chinese culture and, as such, they are far less squeamish about killing, plucking and dressing their poultry than many of us who are used to buying it 'oven-ready'. This creates much more work for the cook but does ensure that the poultry is as fresh as is possible, with all the benefit of flavour that this brings. The French, who are also revered for their food, have a similar attitude to fresh poultry and in both China and France it is very common to see live chickens in cages in the markets.

If you do not want to pursue the traditions of classic Chinese cookery to the extent of plucking your own poultry, the next best flavour will be achieved by using free-range or corn-fed chickens, both of which are now easy to come by both in supermarkets and the better butcher's shops.

An All-Round Winner

Chicken is so versatile. It can be cooked in many different ways, even when the cooking is limited to a hob, and mixed with just about any ingredient. It can be flavoured with the mildest of seasonings and steamed to maximise the natural flavour of the chicken, or it can withstand the boldest of treatments with chillis, peppers and any of the hottest sauces. It is most practical (and economical) to buy a whole chicken and to joint it yourself, which will provide a variety of meats for a variety of dishes – remember, most Chinese recipes use comparatively little meat, combining it with vegetables to make the meat go further. And don't discard the carcass, use it for stock and for so many of the Chinese soups.

Peking Duck – a Brand New Classic

Peking Duck is probably the most famous of all Chinese recipes. As such, it would be more than reasonable to assume that the origins of the dish must be almost lost in history, but this is not so. For one thing, Peking Duck is roasted and, as I have said before, very few homes in China have an oven! So, this great dish was originally only to be found in restaurants and then only from the latter half of the nineteenth century. It is also said to have originated, not in Peking at all, but in Inner Mongolia! Well, whatever the history, it is the most delicious of dishes!

What makes Peking Duck so exceptional amongst duck dishes is its crispy skin. This, in my opinion, makes it stand out from all other duck dishes, Chinese or otherwise.

There are many recipes for duck which sound very similar. The difference is in the preparation and the seasoning of the meat. Sometimes duck is marinated before cooking, and sometimes it is steamed before frying. Interestingly enough, fried duck sound as if it should be very greasy, but it is not at all – the frying takes place at such a high temperature that the duck meat is very crisp but dry once cooking is complete.

SZECHUAN BANG BANG CHICKEN

Bang Bang Chicken should be served in layers from a platter. Everyone should toss their individual helping to mix all the ingredients together before eating.

Serves 4

INGREDIENTS
2 chicken breasts
1 medium cucumber

Sauce
4 tbsps peanut butter
2 tsps sesame oil
½ tsp sugar
¼ tsp salt
2 tsps stock
½ tsp chilli sauce

Simmer the chicken breasts in a pan of water for 30 minutes, then drain and cut them into 1.25cm/½ inch thick slices. Thinly slice the cucumber, or cut it into julienne sticks, making a bed of it on a large serving platter. Pile the shredded chicken on top. Mix the peanut butter with the sesame oil, sugar, salt and stock. Pour the sauce evenly over the chicken and drizzle with the chilli sauce.

SZECHUAN CHILLI CHICKEN

The Szechuan-style heat in this recipe comes from the dried and fresh chillies – use half quantities of both if you think the dish might be too hot!

Serves 4

INGREDIENTS
340g/12oz boneless chicken breasts
1 tsp salt
1 egg white
5 tbsps oil
1½ tbsps cornflour
2 slices fresh root ginger, peeled
2 small dried chillies
2 green or red peppers, seeded
2 fresh chillies, seeded and finely chopped
2 tbsps soy sauce
2 tbsps wine vinegar

Cut the chicken into bite-sized pieces. Add the salt, egg white, 1 tbsp of the oil, and the cornflour. Rub the seasoning evenly over the chicken pieces to form a thin coating.

Chop the ginger and dried chillies and cut the peppers into bite-sized pieces. Heat the remaining oil in a wok. Add the ginger and fresh and dried chillies and stir-fry for 1 minute. Add the chicken pieces, separating them while stirring. Cook until lightly browned. Add the peppers, soy sauce and vinegar and fry for a further 2 minutes. Serve immediately with steamed rice.

STIR-FRIED MINCED CHICKEN ON CRISPY NOODLES

This spicy chicken stir-fry is ideal for serving with crispy noodles. Some supermarkets now sell minced turkey which could be used in place of the chicken, but it is not so authentic.

Serves 4

INGREDIENTS
225g/8oz chicken breasts
2 slices cooked smoked ham
6 slices fresh root ginger, peeled
1 large onion
3 spring onions
3 tbsps oil
½ tsp salt
2 tbsps soy sauce
2 tbsps chicken stock
1 tbsp vinegar
1 tbsp sherry
1 tbsp chilli oil
1 tsp sugar
2 tsps cornflour
2 tbsps water

Mince the chicken, finely shred the ham, ginger and onion, and slice the spring onions. Heat the oil in a large frying-pan or wok, then add the onion, ham and ginger and stir-fry for 2 minutes. Add the minced chicken, sprinkle with salt, soy sauce and stock, then stir-fry for a further 2 minutes. Add vinegar, sherry, chilli oil, sugar, spring onions, and the cornflour blended with 2 tbsps water. Cook over a high heat for 2 minutes until boiling and thickened.

CHICKEN WITH BEAN SPROUTS

The marinade which flavours the chicken then provides the same base for this dish of chicken and bean sprouts.

Serves 4

INGREDIENTS
1 chicken, boned
1 tbsp Chinese wine
1 tsp cornflour
225g/8oz bean sprouts
2 tbsps oil
½ spring onion, finely sliced
1 tsp sugar
280ml/½ pint chicken stock
Salt and freshly ground black
  pepper

Bone the chicken and cut the meat into thin slices or strips. Place the chicken on a plate and pour the Chinese wine over it. Sprinkle with the cornflour and stir well. Leave the chicken to marinate for 30 minutes.

Blanch the bean sprouts in boiling, lightly salted water for 1 minute. Rinse under cold running water and set aside to drain. Remove the chicken from the marinade with a slotted spoon.

Heat the oil in a wok and stir-fry the spring onion and the chicken until browned. Add the drained bean sprouts and the sugar, then stir in the marinade and the stock. Allow the chicken to cook through, which will take approximately 20 minutes. Check the seasoning, adding salt and pepper to taste. Serve immediately.

DEEP-FRIED CHICKEN
WITH LEMON SLICES

*There are many variations on the recipe of Lemon Chicken.
In this recipe the chicken is marinaded and fried before
being added to a lemon sauce.*

Serves 6-8

INGREDIENTS
1.4kg/3lbs boneless chicken
  breasts
6 tbsps cornflour
3 tbsps plain flour
1 green pepper, seeded
1 red pepper, seeded
Oil for deep-frying
2 lemons, thinly sliced and
  freshly chopped parsley ro
  garnish

Chicken Marinade
½ tsp salt
½ tsp white wine
2 tsps light soy sauce
1 tbsp cornflour
1 tbsp water
1 egg yolk
Freshly ground black pepper

Sauce
3 tbsps sugar
3 tbsps lemon juice
6 tbsps chicken or vegetable
  stock
½ tsp salt
2 tbsps cornflour
1 tsp sesame oil

Skin the chicken breasts and cut them into thin, bite-sized pieces. Mix together all the ingredients for the marinade, add the prepared chicken and leave for 10 minutes. Mix the cornflour and flour together on a plate and use to coat the chicken pieces. Combine the ingredients for the sauce in a small bowl. Cut the peppers into 2.5cm/1 inch pieces.

Place a wok over a high heat, add the oil and heat until almost smoking. Deep-fry the chicken slices until golden brown. Remove with a slotted spoon to a heated plate. Pour off all but 1 tbsp of the oil. Stir-fry the peppers until they begin to brown, then add the sauce. Bring to the boil, stirring until thickened. Add the chicken pieces, and stir for a further few minutes. Transfer to a heated serving platter, and garnish with the lemon slices and chopped parsley.

STIR-FRIED CHICKEN WITH YELLOW BEAN SAUCE

Yellow Bean Sauce is one of the many stir-fry sauces readily available in supermarkets everywhere. It is quite salty but not as strong in flavour as some other Chinese sauces. Chinese grocers may offer a whole bean or a crushed bean sauce; supermarkets usually stock the latter.

Serves 4

Ingredients
1 egg white, lightly beaten
1 tbsp cornflour
Salt and freshly ground black pepper
460g/1lb boneless chicken breasts, thinly sliced
1 tbsp rice vinegar
1 tbsp light soy sauce
1 tsp sugar
2 tbsps oil
2 tbsps yellow bean sauce
Spring onion flowers (see recipe for Barbecued Spareribs) to garnish

Mix the lightly beaten egg white with the cornflour and a little salt and pepper. Place the sliced chicken in a bowl and pour the egg mixture over, tossing the chicken until well coated. Set aside in a cool place for at least 1 hour.

Combine the vinegar, soy sauce and sugar in a bowl. Remove the chicken to a plate with a slotted spoon and set the egg mixture aside.

Heat a wok and add the oil. When hot, stir-fry the chicken until lightly browned, then remove it from the wok. Add the yellow bean sauce to the wok and stir-fry for 1 minute, then add the vinegar mixture and stir well. Return the chicken to the wok, and cook gently for 2 minutes. Finally, add the egg mixture and simmer until the sauce boils and thickens, stirring all the time. Garnish with spring onion flowers. Serve immediately with boiled rice.

BRAISED CHICKEN WITH GINGER

I always think of braising as a cooking process in the oven, but the Oriental way is in a pan of stock with the vegetables in the bottom of the pan. It works well, as you will see.

Serves 4

INGREDIENTS
1 chicken, boned
½ tsp chopped fresh root ginger
1 carrot, peeled and diced
1 turnip, peeled and diced
1 courgette, diced
1 onion, thinly sliced
5 slices fresh root ginger, peeled
Salt and freshly ground black
   pepper

Separate the breasts and the leg meat from the boned chicken. Keep each leg in one piece. Place the remaining meat and the bones from the chicken in a saucepan, with just enough water to cover. Boil until the liquid has reduced to a quarter. Strain the stock through a fine sieve.

Sprinkle the chopped ginger on the inside of the 2 pieces of chicken leg meat and season with salt and pepper. Roll up tightly and secure with kitchen string.

Add 150ml/¼ pint water to the chicken stock and bring to the boil in a saucepan. Add the prepared vegetables, sliced ginger, rolled leg meat and the 2 chicken breasts. Cook for approximately 35 minutes or until the chicken is cooked through. Remove the rolled leg meat, cut off the string and cut the meat into rounds. Spread the slices on a warmed serving plate. Take out the chicken breasts and slice them thinly. Arrange the slices on the warmed plate with the leg meat. Remove the vegetables using a slotted spoon, arrange them around the meat and then pour over a little of the stock. Serve piping hot.

CHICKEN LIVERS WITH PEPPERS

The Chinese eat a great deal of chicken and would certainly not waste the livers. This recipe is mild in flavour and could be spiced by adding a pinch of five-spice powder.

Serves 4

INGREDIENTS
4 Chinese dried mushrooms
460g/1lb chicken livers
30g/1oz fresh root ginger
1 tbsp rice vinegar
2 tsps sugar
1 small leek
1 onion
1 green pepper
1 red pepper
3 tbsps vegetable oil
2 spring onion flowers (see recipe for Barbecued Spareribs) to garnish

Soak the mushrooms in hot water for 20 minutes. Trim the chicken livers, and blanch them in boiling water for 3 minutes, then drain and slice. Peel and finely slice the root ginger.

Mix together the vinegar and sugar, add the ginger and set aside. Clean and trim the leek and cut into thin rings or slices. Peel and slice the onion and cut into strips, then seed the peppers, cutting them also into strips. Drain the mushrooms and remove hard stalks, then cut the caps into thin slices.

Heat a wok, add the oil and, when hot, add the mushrooms, onion, leek and peppers, and stir-fry for 5 minutes. Remove the vegetables with a slotted spoon and set aside. Add the sliced livers and ginger mixture to the wok and stir-fry for 5 minutes, then return the vegetables to the wok and heat through. Serve garnished with the spring onion flowers.

LEMON CHICKEN

Lemon Chicken is one of my favourite Oriental dishes – no packet mix can ever touch the exquisite flavour of a homemade sauce! I serve it with broccoli and mangetout, stir-fried and sprinkled with sesame seeds.

Serves 4

INGREDIENTS
90ml/3 fl oz oil for frying
900g/2lbs chicken pieces
Lemon slices to garnish

Lemon Sauce
1 tbsp cornflour
5 tbsps water
Juice 1 lemon
2 tbsps sweet sherry
Pinch of sugar, if required

Heat a wok and add the oil. When hot, add the chicken pieces and turn them in the oil until well browned. Reduce the heat, cover and simmer for 30 minutes, or until the chicken is cooked. Remove the chicken with a slotted spoon and drain on absorbent kitchen paper. Place the chicken pieces in a serving dish and keep them warm in the oven.

Prepare the sauce. Carefully drain the oil from the wok. Mix the cornflour to a paste with 2 tbsps of the water. Place the lemon juice and remaining water in the wok, and bring to the boil. Add the cornflour, and stir until boiling, then simmer for 2 minutes until thickened. Add the sherry and sugar, and simmer for a further 2 minutes. Pour the sauce over the chicken pieces and garnish with lemon slices. Serve with boiled rice.

CHICKEN & CASHEWS

*Cashew nuts always seem to be a really luxurious ingredient,
but they are quite commonplace in Chinese cookery. In this
recipe they retain some of their crunchy texture and contrast
well with the tender pieces of chicken.*

Serves 4

INGREDIENTS

460g/1lb chicken breasts,
    skinned, boned and shredded
150ml/¼ pint chicken stock or
    150ml/¼ pint hot water and 1
    chicken stock cube
4 tsps cornflour
½ tsp five-spice powder
Salt
4 tbsps peanut oil
1 onion, sliced
1 clove garlic, crushed
1 stick celery, thinly sliced
120g/4oz green beans, trimmed
    and sliced
1 carrot, cut into matchsticks
2 spring onions, sliced
1 tbsp light soy sauce
90g/3oz roasted cashews

Simmer the chicken bones in a
little water to make chicken
stock, or dissolve the chicken
stock cube in hot water. Set aside
to cool. Combine half the
cornflour, the five-spice powder
and a pinch of salt, then toss the
shredded chicken in the mixture.

Heat a wok, add the peanut oil
and, when hot, add the chicken
pieces, a few at a time, tossing
them over in the hot oil. Stir-fry
until the chicken just starts to
change colour – about 3 minutes.
Remove the chicken with a
slotted spoon, and drain on
absorbent kitchen paper. Repeat
until all the chicken is cooked.
Carefully pour off all but 1 tbsp
of oil, and add the onion and
garlic, then cook for 2 minutes.
Add the celery, beans, carrot and
spring onions, and stir-fry for a
further 2 minutes. Strain the
chicken stock into the wok and
cook for 3 minutes, until the
vegetables are tender but still
crisp. Mix the remaining
cornflour with 2 tbsps of water,
add the soy sauce and pour the
mixture into the wok. Adjust the
seasoning if necessary. Return to
the boil and let the mixture
simmer for 3 minutes. Add the
chicken and heat through.

Remove the wok from the heat,
stir in the cashews, and serve at
once with noodles or rice.

PEKING EGG BATTERED CHICKEN WITH BEAN SPROUTS, IN ONION AND GARLIC SAUCE

Serve this dish with plain boiled rice and some broccoli stir-fried with other seasonal vegetables. The bean sprouts should be cooked very briefly, so that they remain crisp.

Serves 4

INGREDIENTS
3 boneless chicken breasts
Salt and freshly ground black
  pepper
2 eggs, lightly beaten
2 cloves garlic
2 spring onions
4 tbsps oil
4 tbsps chicken stock
Vinegar to taste
225g/8oz bean sprouts

Cut each chicken breast into very thin 10cm/4 inch slices and rub them with salt and pepper. Beat the eggs lightly, and add the chicken slices. Crush the garlic and cut the spring onions into 2.5cm/1 inch pieces.

Heat the oil in a wok. Add the chicken pieces one by one, then reduce the heat to low. Leave to cook for 1-2 minutes. Once the egg coating has set, sprinkle the chicken with garlic and spring onion. Finally, add the stock and vinegar to taste, then simmer gently for 2 minutes.

Remove the chicken from the wok and cut each slice into small regular pieces. Pour the remaining sauce from the wok over the chicken. Add the bean sprouts to the empty wok, toss in any remaining sauce and stir-fry briefly, just for a few seconds. Make a bed of bean sprouts on a warmed serving platter and serve the chicken in the onion and garlic sauce on top.

STIR-FRIED CHICKEN WITH SLICED COURGETTES

This chicken recipe is very lightly flavoured and is served in a clear cornflour glaze on a bed of fried courgette slices.

Serves 4-6

INGREDIENTS

680g/1½ lbs boneless chicken breasts
2 tsps cornflour
1 egg white
1 tbsp pale dry sherry
1 tsp salt
¼ tsp freshly ground black pepper
225g/8oz courgettes
4 tbsps peanut oil
2 slices fresh root ginger, peeled and shredded

Cut the chicken into thin slices. In a large bowl, mix the chicken with the cornflour, egg white, sherry, salt and pepper. Leave for a few minutes then drain, reserving the marinade. Cut the courgettes into thin slices.

Heat 3 tbsps of the oil in a wok with the ginger. Add the chicken, and stir-fry for 2 minutes, until all the pieces have turned white. Transfer the chicken to a bowl. Wipe the wok clean and add the remaining peanut oil, then stir-fry the courgettes for 2 minutes. Transfer them to a serving platter. Return the chicken to the wok, add the cornflour mixture and stir for a few seconds until boiling and a clear glaze is formed. Pour the contents of the wok into the middle of the courgettes. Serve at once.

CHICKEN LIVERS WITH CHINESE LEAVES & ALMONDS

Chicken livers require only light flavourings and seasonings, which will not mask their own delicate flavour. The crunchy texture of the fried almonds contrasts well with the soft, moist livers.

Serves 4

INGREDIENTS

225g/8oz chicken livers
3 tbsps oil
60g/2oz split blanched almonds
1 clove garlic
60g/2oz mangetout
8-10 Chinese leaves, finely shredded
2 tsps cornflour mixed with 1 tbsp cold water
2 tbsps soy sauce
150ml/¼ pint chicken stock

Pick over the chicken livers and remove any discoloured areas or tubes. Cut the livers into even-sized pieces. Heat a wok and pour in the oil. When the oil is hot, turn the heat down and add the almonds. Cook over a gentle heat, stirring continuously, until golden brown. Remove the almonds and drain on absorbent kitchen paper.

Add the garlic to the wok, cook for 1-2 minutes to flavour the oil then remove the garlic and discard. Add the chicken livers and cook for about 2-3 minutes, stirring frequently. Remove the livers and set aside. Add the mangetout to the wok and stir-fry for 1 minute then add the Chinese leaves and cook for 1 minute. Remove the vegetables and set them aside. Mix together the cornflour and water with the soy sauce and stock. Pour into the wok and bring to the boil. Cook until thickened and clear. Return all the other ingredients to the sauce and reheat for 30 seconds. Serve immediately.

CHICKEN WITH WALNUTS & CELERY

Oyster sauce is one of my favourite strong Chinese flavourings. The addition of walnuts to this stir-fry makes an unusual dish.

Serves 4

INGREDIENTS

225g/8oz boneless chicken, cut into 2.5cm/1 inch pieces
2 tbsps soy sauce
2 tsps brandy
1 tsp cornflour
Salt and freshly grated black pepper
2 tbsps oil
1 clove garlic
120g/4oz walnut halves
3 sticks celery, cut in diagonal slices
2 tsps oyster sauce
150ml/¼ pint water or chicken stock

Combine the chicken with the soy sauce, brandy, cornflour, salt and pepper. Heat a wok and add the oil and garlic. Cook for about 1 minute to flavour the oil, then remove and discard the garlic. Add half the chicken and stir-fry quickly without allowing it to brown. Remove the chicken then add the remainder and cook as before. Remove the cooked chicken. Add the walnuts to the wok and cook for about 2 minutes, until lightly browned and crisp. Add the celery to the wok and cook for about 1 minute, then add the oyster sauce and water and bring to the boil. When boiling, return the chicken to the pan and stir to coat all the ingredients well. Serve immediately.

CHICKEN WITH CLOUD EARS

Chinese mushrooms have wonderful names! Unless you can get to a Chinese supermarket you may have difficulty buying specific varieties of dried Oriental mushrooms, but any type may be used for this recipe.

Serves 4

INGREDIENTS

12 cloud ears, wood ears or other Chinese dried mushrooms, soaked in boiling water for 5 minutes
460g/1lb chicken breasts, boned and thinly sliced
1 egg white
2 tsps cornflour
2 tsps white wine
2 tsps sesame oil
2.5cm/1 inch piece fresh root ginger, peeled and left whole
1 clove garlic, left whole
280ml/½ pint oil
280ml/½ pint chicken stock
1 tbsp cornflour
3 tbsps light soy sauce
Salt and freshly ground black pepper

Soak the mushrooms until they soften and swell. Remove all the skin and bone from the chicken and cut the meat into thin slices. Mix the chicken with the egg white, 2 tsps cornflour, wine and sesame oil. Heat a wok for a few minutes then pour in the oil for frying. Add the whole piece of ginger and whole garlic clove to the oil and cook for about 1 minute. Remove and discard the ginger and garlic and reduce the heat. Add about a quarter of the chicken at a time to the wok and stir-fry each batch for 1 minute. Remove the cooked pieces and continue cooking until all the chicken is fried.

Remove all but 2 tbsps of the oil from the wok. Drain the mushrooms and squeeze them to extract all the liquid. If using mushrooms with stems, remove and discard the stems before slicing the caps thinly. Cut cloud ears or wood ears into small pieces. Add the mushrooms to the wok and cook for about 1 minute, then add the stock and allow it to come almost to the boil. Mix together the 1 tbsp of cornflour and the soy sauce and add a spoonful of the hot stock. Add the mixture to the wok, stirring constantly, and bring to the boil. Allow to boil for 1-2 minutes or until thickened. The sauce will clear when the cornflour has cooked sufficiently. Return the chicken to the wok and add salt and pepper. Stir thoroughly for about 1 minute and serve immediately.

CHICKEN IN
HOT PEPPER SAUCE

You can make this sauce as hot as you like simply by adding more chilli sauce. Taste after each addition – you can always add more, but you can never take any away!

Serves 4

INGREDIENTS
1 chicken
2 tbsps oil
2-3 cloves garlic, chopped
1 green pepper, seeded and cut into thin strips
1 red pepper, seeded and cut into thin strips
1 tsp wine vinegar
1 tbsp light soy sauce
1 tsp sugar
280ml/½ pint chicken stock
1 tbsp chilli sauce
Salt and freshly ground black pepper

First bone the chicken completely and cut all the meat into thin strips. Heat the oil in a wok and stir-fry the garlic, chicken and the green and red peppers for about 15 minutes, until the chicken is cooked. Pour off any excess oil and add the vinegar. Boil until almost evaporated, then stir in the soy sauce, sugar and stock. Gradually add the chilli sauce, tasting after each addition. Season with a little salt and pepper to taste. Cook until the sauce has reduced slightly. Serve piping hot.

CHICKEN BREASTS WITH SPRING ONION

Steamed chicken is deliciously moist and tender – it is an excellent way of cooking chicken breasts which can be very dry and slightly tough. The chicken is served with a very lightly flavoured sauce made of reduced stock and soy sauce.

Serves 4

INGREDIENTS

1 spring onion, sliced
1 carrot, cut into thin julienne strips
2-3 cloves garlic, chopped
4 chicken breasts
Salt and freshly ground black pepper
175ml/6 fl oz chicken stock
1 tbsp soy sauce
½ tsp sugar
1 tsp cornflour, combined with a little water

Mix together the spring onion, carrot and half the garlic. Slice the chicken breasts open lengthways, along the side, without cutting through them completely. Season the insides with salt and pepper and fill each breast with ¼ of the vegetable stuffing. Pull the top half of the breast back into place. Season again with salt and pepper. Steam the stuffed chicken breasts for approximately 15 minutes, until cooked through.

Bring the stock to the boil in a small saucepan. Stir in the soy sauce, sugar and the remaining garlic, simmer and allow to reduce for a few minutes. Thicken the sauce by adding the cornflour paste and stirring continuously until boiling and thickened. Cut the stuffed chicken breasts into slices and serve them topped with sauce.

STUFFED CHICKEN LEGS

Boning chicken legs is not too difficult a task providing you have a small sharp knife. Remove any white sinews as well, as these are tough and unpleasant to eat. Boneless chicken thighs may be prepared in the same way, although their shape will not be quite so neat.

Serves 4

INGREDIENTS
6-8 Chinese dried black
   mushrooms, soaked for 15
   minutes in warm water
4 chicken legs, boned
1 egg, beaten
½ tsp finely chopped fresh root
   ginger
280ml/½ pint chicken stock
½ tsp sugar
Salt and freshly ground black
   pepper
1 tsp cornflour, combined with a
   little water

Drain the mushrooms and cut them into thin slices. Flatten out each piece of leg meat and brush a little beaten egg over the inside. Divide the mushroom slices evenly between the 4 pieces of meat and sprinkle with half the ginger. Roll up and secure with thin kitchen string. Steam the stuffed chicken rolls for approximately 25 minutes, or until cooked.

Bring the stock to the boil in a pan and allow to reduce by half. Add the remaining ginger and the sugar and season with salt and pepper to taste. Add the cornflour paste to the sauce and heat, stirring continuously, until boiling and thickened. Serve the chicken rolls sliced into rounds and topped with the sauce.

CHICKEN WITH LEMON & GINGER SAUCE

Using a whole chicken for this recipe is more economical than buying prepared boneless breast fillets. However, if you prefer to buy the fillets you will need 4 pieces, weighing about 680g/1½ lbs in total.

Serves 4

INGREDIENTS

1 lemon, washed
6-8 Chinese dried black
  mushrooms, soaked for 15
  minutes in warm water
2 tbsps oil
1 chicken, boned and the meat
  cut into thin slices
1 tsp chopped fresh root ginger
1 tsp wine vinegar
1 tbsp soy sauce
280ml/½ pint chicken stock
½ tsp sugar
Salt and freshly ground black
  pepper

Peel the lemon with a potato peeler, and cut the peel into thin julienne strips. Blanch in boiling water for a few seconds and set aside to drain. Squeeze and reserve the juice of the lemon. Cook the mushrooms in boiling, lightly salted water for 15 minutes and then rinse them in cold water. Drain the mushrooms thoroughly, and slice them thinly.

Heat the oil in a wok and stir-fry the chicken, ginger and lemon peel for 2 minutes. Pour off any excess fat and add the vinegar to the wok, heating until it has almost evaporated. Stir in the lemon juice, soy sauce, stock, sugar and mushrooms. Reduce the heat and cook for 5 minutes. Season with salt and pepper to taste and serve hot.

PEKING DUCK

This world-famous dish is a particular favourite of mine. Not only do the crisp skin, succulent meat and tangy sauce make a wonderful combination, the messy process of filling the pancakes adds to the enjoyment. Although we tend to eat all the ingredients together, traditionally only the skin was eaten with the pancakes, cucumber and spring onion, while the duck was carved and served as a second course.

Serves 6

INGREDIENTS
1 duck, weighing 2.3kg/5lbs

Glaze
5 tbsps maltose (malt sugar) or thick honey
4-5 tbsps boiling water
1 tbsp soy sauce

Duck Sauce (makes about 570ml/1 pint)
3 tbsps sesame oil
175g/6oz sweet bean paste or hoisin sauce
175g/6oz sugar
175g/6 fl oz water

Mandarin Pancakes (makes 30)
460g/1lb plain flour
370ml/13 fl oz water
Sesame oil

To serve
1 large cucumber
12 spring onions

To prepare the duck, wipe the insides with damp kitchen paper, but do not wet the skin. Place the duck on a wire rack in a sink and pour over a kettleful of boiling water. Pat the duck with ▶

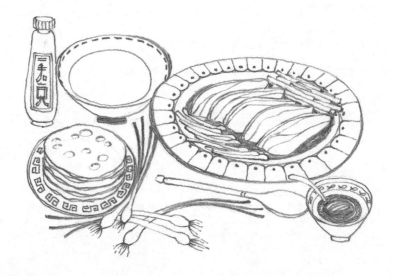

absorbent kitchen paper to remove any excess moisture and transfer the duck to another rack over a tray. Mix the glaze ingredients together and brush all over the duck. Coat the inside of the duck as well. Leave the duck to dry for about 1 hour, or until the glaze has dried, then paint with another layer of the glaze and leave to dry again. Repeat until the glaze is used up. If possible, hang the duck on two meat hooks tucked under the wings (otherwise leave the duck on the wire rack), and leave in a cool airy place overnight, (a pantry would be excellent) to allow the skin to dry completely. Do not pierce the skin.

To make the duck sauce, heat the oil in a pan, add the sweet bean paste, sugar and water and mix together until well blended. Simmer for 2-3 minutes, or until the sauce thickens. Pour into a bowl and leave to cool, then refrigerate until required.

To prepare the pancakes, sieve the flour into a mixing bowl and make a well in the centre. Bring 280ml/½ pint of the water to a rolling boil and pour into the flour. Quickly stir the flour, a little at a time, into the water, using the handle of a wooden spoon. When well mixed, stir in the rest of the cold water and mix to a dough. Turn out on to a lightly floured surface and knead for 5-6 minutes until the dough is smooth. Cover the dough with plastic wrap and leave to rest for 15-20 minutes.

Knead the dough again for a few more minutes until smooth. Divide into two evenly-sized pieces, then roll each piece out into a long sausage shape and cut into a total of 30 equal pieces. Working with two pieces of dough at a time, roll each piece into a ball. Keep the rest of the dough covered to prevent it from drying out. Flatten all the dough balls into circles using your hands. Using a pastry brush, paint half the circles with sesame oil on one side. Sandwich the other circles on top of the oiled surfaces to make 15 pairs. Keep each pair as evenly-sized as possible and, on a lightly floured surface, roll out one pair at a time until they are wafer thin and almost transparent. The circles should be about 16.5cm/6½ inches in diameter. Repeat with the remaining dough.

Heat a heavy-based, non-stick frying pan or griddle over a medium heat. Wipe the surface with an oiled cloth and place one pair of pancakes in the pan. Cook for 1-2 minutes or until brown spots appear on the underside. Turn the pancakes over and cook the other side until the surface starts to puff up. Remove from the pan and separate the two pancakes while they are stil hot. Stack up on a plate and keep covered to prevent them from drying out.

Preheat the oven to 190°C/375°F/Gas Mark 5. To cook the duck, place it on a rack over a roasting pan and roast in the middle of the preheated oven for 30 minutes. Turn the duck over using two wooden spoons so that you don't pierce the skin, and roast for a further 20 minutes. Turn the duck back over again and continue roasting for 20-30 minutes, or until the skin is dark brown and crispy. If the skin starts to look too brown too soon, reduce the oven temperature to 160°C/325°F/Gas Mark 3, then raise it again to 220°C/425°F/Gas Mark 7 for the last 10-15 minutes.

While the duck is cooking, cut

the spring onions into thin strips and slice the cucumber into thin batons. To reheat the pancakes, place batches in a steamer over boiling water for 5-10 minutes. Alternatively, wait until the duck is cooked and reheat them in the oven.

Remove the duck from the oven and let it stand for 10 minutes before carving. (If wished, the pancakes can now be reheated in the oven, wrapped in foil, at the reduced temperature of 180°C/350°F/Gas Mark 4.) Cut the skin into pieces then carve the meat. Serve with the pancakes, spring onions and cucumber and the duck sauce.

DUCK WITH
CORIANDER SAUCE

One of the best things about duck, in my opinion, is the crispy skin, so I particularly like recipes such as this which utilise the skin as a garnish.

Serves 4

INGREDIENTS

1 duck, boned, leg and breast meat reserved (use the bones and remaining meat for stock)
1 spring onion
60g/2oz bamboo shoots, blanched
2 Chinese dried mushrooms, soaked for 15 minutes in warm water and drained
10 coriander seeds
280ml/½ pint duck stock
1 tsp cornflour, combined with a little water
Salt and freshly ground black pepper
3 tbsps oil

Skin the duck breasts and reserve both the meat and skin. Chop the following ingredients separately in a food processor: one duck breast, then the spring onion, the bamboo shoots and the Chinese mushrooms. Mix all the processed ingredients together in a small bowl to make a stuffing. Spread the stuffing mixture on to the boned leg meat and the remaining duck breast. Roll the meat around the stuffing and wrap each duck parcel in foil. Twist the ends to seal well. Steam the duck rolls in a steamer for 35 minutes.

Crush the coriander seeds and place in a small saucepan. Add the duck stock and cook over a gentle heat until reduced by one quarter. Thicken, if necessary, with the cornflour, stirring continuously until boiling and thickened. Season to taste with salt and pepper. Heat the oil in a frying pan and fry the reserved duck skin until crisp. Leave to cool and then cut into small pieces. Remove the foil from the duck. Serve the rolls sliced into rounds, with some of the crispy skin and the sauce.

DUCKLING WITH CASHEW NUTS

I love cashew nuts so I tend to use a few more than the recipe says, and to cut them quite coarsely, to obtain a crunchy texture. Walnuts or pecan nuts would also work well in this recipe.

Serves 4

INGREDIENTS
20 raw cashew nut halves
2 tbsps oil
2 cloves garlic, finely chopped
1 duckling, boned and the meat
   cut into slices
1 spring onion, chopped
2 tbsps soy sauce
225ml/8 fl oz chicken stock
½ tsp vinegar
1 tsp sugar
Salt and freshly ground black
   pepper

Slice the cashew nuts into thin strips, using a very sharp knife. Heat the oil in a wok and stir-fry the garlic and duckling until the meat is sealed and browned. Add the cashew nuts and the spring onion and stir-fry for 1 minute. Pour off any excess fat from the wok. Stir in the soy sauce, then the stock, vinegar and sugar. Season with salt and pepper. Continue cooking until the duckling is tender and the sauce has reduced enough to lightly coat the pieces of meat.

DUCKLING WITH ONIONS

This recipe, which sounds and tastes luxurious, is simple and quick to prepare. The sauce is rich and full of flavour, so serve the duckling with boiled rice and a plain Oriental vegetable stir-fry.

Serves 4

INGREDIENTS

2 tbsps oil
2 large onions, finely sliced
1 duckling, boned and the meat cut into slices
2 tbsps Chinese wine
1 tbsp soy sauce
1 tbsp hoisin sauce
280ml/½ pint chicken stock
Salt and freshly ground black pepper

Heat the oil in a wok and stir-fry the onions until lightly browned. Ease the onions up the side of the wok out of the oil, to keep them warm. Add the duckling to the wok and stir-fry until lightly browned. Pour in the Chinese wine. Push the onions back into the bottom of the wok, with the duckling, and stir in the soy sauce, hoisin sauce and the stock. Allow to cook until slightly reduced, then season with salt and pepper and serve immediately.

AROMATIC AND CRISPY DUCK

I once overheard a customer in a Chinese restaurant trying to get to the bottom of the differences between all the varieties of crispy duck! This one is steamed before frying, which makes the meat very tender. It is aromatic from being rubbed with sauces and spices.

Serves 4

INGREDIENTS
1 duck, weighing 1.6kg/3½ lbs
2 tbsps black bean sauce
2 tbsps dark soy sauce
2 tsps five-spice powder
3 slices fresh root ginger
Oil for deep-frying
Mandarin pancakes, (see recipe for Peking Duck)
Duck sauce, (see recipe for Peking Duck)
½ cucumber, shredded
4 spring onions, shredded

Rub the duck inside and out with the black bean sauce, soy sauce, five-spice powder and ginger. Leave in a cool place overnight.

Place the duck in a steamer and steam vigorously for 1½ hours, then drain and dry the duck. Heat some oil for deep-frying in a wok or large saucepan. Deep-fry the duck for 10-12 minutes until very crispy. Scrape the duck meat off the carcass. Roll up in the pancakes with duck sauce, shredded cucumber and spring onions.

DUCK WITH
BAMBOO SHOOTS

Bamboo shoots require a great deal of preparation when they are fresh. The canned shoots loose a little of the crisp texture of the fresh vegetable but are very convenient to use. They provide more texture than flavour and help to make a little meat go a long way!

Serves 4

INGREDIENTS
225g/8oz bamboo shoots, cut into thin slices
90g/3oz sugar
150ml/¼ pint water
1 tsp chopped fresh root ginger
1 tbsp hoisin sauce
2 duck breasts
1 tbsp oil
Salt and freshly ground black pepper

Preheat the oven to 220°C/425°F/Gas Mark 7. If using fresh bamboo shoots, cook them in boiling, lightly salted water for approximately 15 minutes. Drain thoroughly and set aside. Mix the sugar and water together in a small saucepan, stirring thoroughly. Add the ginger and the hoisin sauce. Place over a gentle heat and cook until a light syrup is formed. Brush this syrup liberally over the duck breasts.

Heat the oil in a frying pan and add the duck breasts, skin-side down. Sear on each side. Remove from the oil and finish cooking in the hot oven, for approximately 15 minutes. Shortly before the duck breasts are cooked, stir-fry the bamboo shoots in the oil used to sear the duck breasts. Season with salt and pepper and serve hot with the duck breasts, sliced.

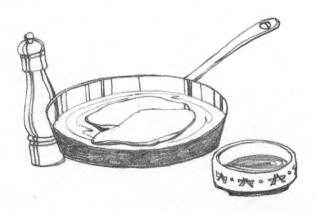

DUCKLING IN FIVE-SPICE SAUCE

The aromatic spiciness of five-spice powder, combined with the crunchy texture of water chestnuts, makes a wonderful combination with duck meat.

Serves 4

INGREDIENTS
12 canned water chestnuts
120g/4oz bamboo shoots
1 tbsp sesame oil
1 tsp chopped fresh root ginger
1 duckling, boned and the meat cut into thin slices
4 Chinese dried mushrooms, soaked in warm water for 15 minutes, drained and chopped
280ml/½ pint duck stock
1 tsp five-spice powder
Salt and freshly ground black pepper
1 tsp cornflour, combined with a little water

Rinse the water chestnuts and blanch in boiling, lightly salted water for 10 minutes. Lift out with a slotted spoon and set them aside to drain. Blanch the bamboo shoots in the same water, rinse and then drain. Once well-drained, cut them into thin matchsticks.

Heat the sesame oil in a wok and stir-fry the ginger and the duckling slices. Remove the ginger and duckling with a slotted spoon and stir-fry the bamboo shoots, chopped Chinese mushrooms and water chestnuts. Pour off any excess fat from the wok and return the duckling and the ginger to the wok with the vegetables. Add the duck stock and stir well. Sprinkle with the five-spice powder and allow to cook for approximately 15 minutes. Check the seasoning, adding salt and pepper as necessary. Thicken the sauce by stirring in the cornflour paste, stirring continuously until boiling and thickened. Serve hot.

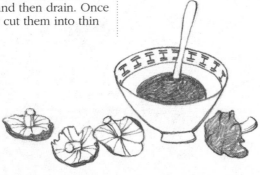

LACQUERED DUCK

*A honey and soy sauce glaze or marinade gives such a rich,
deep colour and gloss to this dish – it is easy to see where the
title 'lacquered' is derived from.*

Serves 4

INGREDIENTS
½ tsp soy sauce
1 tbsp honey
1 tsp five-spice powder
1 tsp wine vinegar
2 cloves garlic, finely chopped
1 tsp cornflour, combined with a
    little water
2 duck breasts
Salt and freshly ground black
    pepper

To make the marinade, mix together the soy sauce and the honey, add the five-spice powder and stir well. Stir in the vinegar, garlic and cornflour. Season the breasts with a little salt and pepper and place in an ovenproof dish. Pour the marinade over to coat the duck breasts entirely. Leave to marinate for 24 hours.

Preheat an oven to 220°C/425°F/Gas Mark 7 and cook the duck for approximately 20 minutes, basting frequently with the marinade. To caramelize the tops, place under a hot grill for several minutes until crisp. Watch carefully to prevent the duck breasts from burning.

DUCK WITH GINGER SAUCE

This is a good way of using up duck legs. People always plump for the breast but there is quite a bit of meat on the legs! The slightly citrus flavour of the fresh ginger complements the duck so well.

Serves 4

INGREDIENTS
4 duck legs
10 slices fresh root ginger, peeled
2 tbsps oil
1 spring onion, chopped
2 cloves garlic, finely chopped
1 tbsp soy sauce
280ml/½ pint duck stock
1 tsp cornflour, combined with a
  little water
Salt and freshly ground black
  pepper

Chop off the ends of the duck legs and discard. Using a small sharp knife, slide the blade down the sides of the thigh bone and ease away all the meat. Cut the meat into large slices. Cut the slices of ginger into fine julienne strips and place a little ginger on each slice of meat, then roll up and tie securely with thin kitchen string.

Heat the oil in a wok and stir-fry the spring onion with the garlic. Add the duck rolls, together with any leftover duck meat and fry for 2 minutes. Pour off any excess fat from the wok. Stir in the soy sauce, any leftover ginger and the stock. Simmer for about 20 minutes, until the duck has cooked through completely. Thicken the sauce with the cornflour paste if necessary. Check the seasoning, adding salt and pepper as required. Cut the string from each duck roll and serve hot, with the sauce.

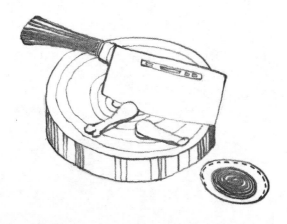

DUCKLING SALAD WITH SWEET & SOUR SAUCE

This is a simple but delicious salad. Garnish with sculptured vegetables if you are artistic and creative! This salad could also be served as a starter, in which case it would serve 4 people.

Serves 2

INGREDIENTS

1 cooked duckling, cooled and boned
½ cucumber
2 carrots
2 tbsps white wine vinegar
1 tsp mustard
1 tsp sugar
1 tbsp soy sauce
4 tsps hoisin sauce
1 tsp sesame oil
1 tbsp peanut oil
Salt and freshly ground black pepper

Cut the duckling meat into bite-sized chunks, cut the cucumber into thin slices, and the carrots into thin julienne strips. Whisk together the vinegar, mustard and sugar in a small bowl. Add the soy sauce, followed by the hoisin sauce. Lastly, whisk in the sesame and peanut oils and season with salt and pepper to taste.

Divide the duckling meat and the vegetables evenly between individual plates, pour a little of the sauce over each portion and serve.

DUCK WITH MANGOES

*The beautiful, aromatic flavour of the mangoes helps to
counteract any excess fattiness in the duck and provides a
perfect blend of ingredients. Mangoes will be heavily
perfumed when they are ripe for eating.*

Serves 4

INGREDIENTS
2 ripe mangoes
280ml/½ pint duck stock
2 duck breasts
3 cloves garlic, finely chopped
1 tsp finely chopped fresh root
  ginger
Salt and freshly ground black
  pepper
2 tbsps oil
1 tsp vinegar
1 tbsp freshly chopped chives

Preheat an oven to
220°C/425°F/Gas Mark 7. Peel the
mangoes. Using a sharp knife,
remove the two cheeks of fruit
from each mango, then cut them
into slices. Blend the slices from
half a mango with the stock in a
liquidiser or food processor until
smooth.

Rub the duck breasts with the
garlic and ginger and season
with salt and pepper. Heat the oil
in a frying pan or wok and seal
the duck breasts all over.
Remove the duck breasts from
the frying pan and finish cooking
on a baking sheet in the
preheated oven for 15-20
minutes.

Reduce the mango stock mixture
by half with the vinegar by
boiling it rapidly in a small
saucepan, adding salt and
pepper to taste. Heat the
remaining mango slices in a
steamer for 1 minute. Slice the
duck breasts and serve them with
the hot mango slices topped with
the sauce. Sprinkle with the
chives just before serving.

DEEP-FRIED BONELESS DUCK

Another variation on crispy spiced duck! This recipe calls for the duck to be simmered in a spiced stock before being fried. Take the cooked duck meat from the bones in large pieces before frying.

Serves 4

INGREDIENTS

1 duck weighing 1.6kg/3½ lbs
1 egg, lightly beaten
4 tbsps cornflour
2 tbsps plain flour
150ml/¼ pint soy sauce
340ml/12 fl oz beef stock
4 cloves garlic
3 tsps five-spice powder
3-4 pieces star anise
Oil for deep-frying
1 crisp lettuce, separated into leaves
½ quantity Duck Sauce (see recipe for Peking Duck)

Simmer the whole duck in a large pan of boiling water for 4-5 minutes, then drain the duck on a rack. Mix the egg, cornflour and flour to a smooth batter.

Mix the soy sauce, stock, garlic and five-spice powder together, then simmer with the star anise for 3-4 minutes in a large pan. Add the duck, and coat well with the sauce. Simmer for 40 minutes, turning the bird over every 10 minutes. Remove the duck from the pan and drain thoroughly. Remove the meat from the bones of the duck and coat it in the batter mixture.

Heat the oil for deep-frying in a wok or saucepan. Deep-fry the duck meat for 3-4 minutes, until very crispy. Cut into 5cm/2 inch pieces. Arrange the meat on a serving platter. Eat, wrapped in crisp lettuce leaves with the Duck Sauce.

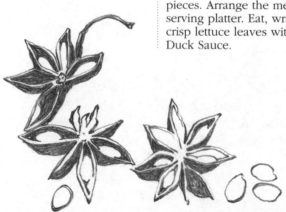

PORK, BEEF & LAMB

To the vast majority of Chinese meat is pork!

Meat is Pork!

Pigs are farmed throughout China, but especially in the south, in the Canton region. In the late 1980s there were about 335 million pigs in China, representing more than 40 per cent of the world's total pig population. It will therefore come as very little surprise that pork is the most widely eaten meat in the country!

As with all Chinese cuisine the cooking time, even for meat dishes, is very short, so most meat is cooked off the bone and minced, shredded or very finely sliced. Of course, the better cuts are particularly suitable for cooking in this way and many

143

of the pork recipes in this chapter call for lean, comparatively expensive cuts such as tenderloin. This does not mean that Chinese cookery is expensive as very little meat is used in each dish, and it is made to go that little bit further by the addition of vegetables.

Some recipes call for joints of meat and a long slow cooking time; Shanghai Long-Cooked Knuckle of Pork is one such dish which takes an economical cut of pork and simmers it for 2 hours, producing a meltingly tender result.

Beef, the Perfect Partner for Strong Flavours

Beef is the second most widely used meat in China and is often associated with strong seasonings and spicy sauces. Beef is eaten throughout China and is frequently cooked in oyster sauce (one of my favourite dishes). I find the marriage of beef with the sauce to be one of the most successful and simplest ways of producing a really savoury and tasty meal.

As with pork, it is the leanest and more luxurious cuts of beef that are most frequently used for Chinese cookery but a little goes a long way and only small quantities of meat will be required for each recipe.

Lamb, a Relatively Rare Treat

Lamb is eaten far less frequently than pork or beef, and also more rarely than fish or shellfish. It is seldom found on restaurant menus in the west, so the delicious lamb recipes that are included in this chapter will probably be as much of a surprise to you as they were to me when I first read about them. Stir-Fried Lamb with Sesame Seeds is lightly caramelised before the sesame seeds are sprinkled over the lamb, and there is also a delicious recipe for lamb's kidneys with asparagus.

It is surprising that there are actually more sheep than cattle in China! I haven't yet got to the bottom of what happens to the ones that are not eaten! Perhaps there have to be more recipes for beef than for lamb because the animals are larger?

Goats, Game and other meats

Goats are raised in many country areas by nomadic herdsmen and there are many classic recipes for goat meat. However, this is not as popular in the cities and major centres of population as lamb, and many good goat recipes have been amended and adapted to use lamb, which is less strong in flavour and more tender. Deer are to be found in the far north of the country and there are also a few in the south, so venison is also used in regional country cooking.

Meat in the Menu

The Chinese have a vast repertoire of meat dishes in their classic cuisine, and yet they are considered to be a very healthy people because they do not eat as much meat as we do in the west. What they do eat they enjoy, producing an enormous variety of dishes by combining the meat with a vast selection of vegetables and seasonings. Many dieticians would recommend that we in the west should adopt a similar style of eating.

When planning a Chinese menu for a family meal for four people it is generally recommended to serve one or two soups and four or five other dishes, at least two of which should be meat. Choose different meats if possible, one pork and one beef, which will balance with a chicken dish, some fish and some vegetables. Choose one meat dish that is hot and spicy and one with a lighter flavour, and try to ensure that two different cooking methods are used for the dishes selected, to give variety in flavour and texture. You don't want everything to be crispy, fried and in a cornflour thickened sauce!

PORK IN SWEET &
SOUR SAUCE

*The most popular sweet and sour pork dish has the pork
coated in batter and fried before it is added to the sauce.
This recipe is simpler to prepare as the meat is just stir-fried
before the sauce is added.*

Serves 4

INGREDIENTS
1 onion
¼ cucumber
½ red pepper, seeded
½ green pepper, seeded
1 slice pineapple, fresh or
  canned
4 tbsps pineapple juice
3 tbsps wine vinegar
1 tsp chilli sauce
1 tbsp sugar
½ tomato, skinned, seeded and
  crushed
340ml/12 fl oz chicken stock
2 tbsps oil
460g/1lb pork, cut into thin strips
1 clove garlic, chopped
1 tsp cornflour, mixed with 1 tsp
  water
Salt and freshly ground black
  pepper

Cut the onion, cucumber, red
and green peppers and
pineapple into thin matchsticks.
Mix together the pineapple juice,
vinegar, chilli sauce, sugar,
crushed tomato and chicken
stock.

Heat the oil in a wok, then stir-
fry the pork and the garlic. Once
the meat is golden brown,
remove it with a slotted spoon
and set aside. Add all the
vegetables and the pineapple to
the wok and stir-fry for 2
minutes. Return the pork to the
wok with the vegetables and
pineapple and pour in the sauce
mixture. Cook for 3-4 minutes,
stirring, and shaking the wok
from time to time. Thicken the
sauce by adding the cornflour
paste, and stir continuously until
boiling and thickened. Season to
taste with salt and pepper. Serve
piping hot.

SZECHUAN 'YU HSIANG' PORK RIBBONS, QUICK-FRIED WITH SHREDDED VEGETABLES

This dish is hot in typically Szechuan style! If you cannot get authentic Szechuan pickles use a hot Indian pickle or an Indonesian pepper sambal – it's not the same, but it still makes your nose tingle!

Serves 4

INGREDIENTS
340g/12oz lean pork
3 slices fresh root ginger, peeled
2 cloves garlic
4 tbsps Szechuan pickles
120g/4oz mangetout
120g/4oz white cabbage
1 red pepper, seeded
2 young carrots
2 dried chillies
4 tbsps oil
120g/4oz bean sprouts
1 tsp salt
4 tbsps stock
3 tsps sesame oil

Sauce
3 tbsps soy sauce
2 tbsps Hoisin sauce
1 tbsp chilli sauce
2 tbsps vinegar

Cut the pork into very thin slices, then cut it again into 2.5cm/1 inch strips. Cut the ginger, garlic, pickle, mangetout, cabbage, pepper, carrots and chillies into small slices. Mix together the ingredients for the sauce.

Heat the 4 tbsps oil in a wok. When hot, add the chillies, pickle, pork and ginger. Stir over a high heat for 2 minutes. Add all the shredded vegetables and the bean sprouts. Sprinkle with salt, and stir over the heat for 2 minutes. Add the stock and cook for a further 2 minutes. Add the sauce ingredients and sesame oil, and continue stir-frying for a further 2 minutes. Serve on a well heated platter with steamed rice.

STIR-FRIED SLICED PORK WITH PIGS' LIVER AND KIDNEY

This recipe makes good use of both pigs' liver and kidney, mixing them with lean pork meat, mangetouts and water chestnuts.

Serves 4

INGREDIENTS
1 pig's kidney
120g/4oz lean pork loin
120g/4oz pigs' liver
120g/4oz mangetout
6 water chestnuts
5 tbsps oil
1 spring onion, finely sliced

Marinade
1½ tbsps white wine
1½ tbsps soy sauce
1½ tbsps cornflour
1 tsp sugar

Sauce
½ tsp freshly ground black pepper
½ tsp vinegar
1 tsp cornflour
½ tsp salt
½ tsp sugar
½ tsp sesame oil
2 tbsps water

Soak the kidney in cold water for 30 minutes, then skin it and remove the core. Cut the pork, liver and kidney into thin slices. Prepare the marinade for the meats by mixing all the ingredients together. Divide between three separate bowls and marinate the pork, liver and kidney separately for 30 minutes. Thinly shred the mangetouts and slice the water chestnuts.

Mix the ingredients for the sauce together, and set aside. Set a wok over a high heat for 30 seconds and pour in 4 tbsps of the oil. Heat until almost smoking, then reduce the heat slightly and stir in the pork, liver and kidney. Stir-fry for 2-3 minutes, then remove the meats with a slotted spoon. Add the remaining 1 tbsp of oil to the wok. Stir-fry the mangetouts and water chestnuts for 1-2 minutes, then add the sauce mixture. If the mixture becomes too thick, add more water. Cook until a thick, transparent paste is formed, then stir in the pork, liver and kidney. Add the spring onion and turn onto a warmed serving dish. Serve immediately.

MEATBALLS WITH BAMBOO SHOOTS

Chopped chives bring freshness to this dish. Do not chop them until just before using, or they will lose much of their impact and punchiness. Dried chives just aren't the same!

Serves 4

INGREDIENTS
225g/8oz boneless chicken
225g/8oz lean pork
1 clove garlic, chopped
1 tbsp freshly chopped chives
1 egg, lightly beaten
Salt and freshly ground black
  pepper
400g/14oz bamboo shoots
2 tbsps oil
1 spring onion, chopped
½ tsp chopped fresh root ginger
175ml/6 fl oz chicken stock
1 tsp cornflour, combined with a
  little water

Mince the chicken and pork in a food processor or mincer with half of the garlic and chives. Place the meat in a bowl and add the egg. Beat well with a fork, and season with salt and pepper. Cut the bamboo shoots into thin, even slices and blanch in boiling, salted water. Rinse under cold water and drain.

Heat 1 tbsp of the oil in a frying pan or wok. Shape the meat in your hands to form small, flat rounds and fry on both sides until almost cooked. Heat the remaining oil in a separate wok and stir-fry the spring onion, remaining garlic and chives, the ginger and bamboo shoots for 2 minutes. Stir in the chicken stock and allow to reduce. Season again with salt and pepper and add the cornflour paste, stirring continuously until the sauce boils and thickens. Cut the meat rounds into evenly-sized strips and finish cooking them in a Chinese steamer. Serve the meat with the bamboo shoots and sauce.

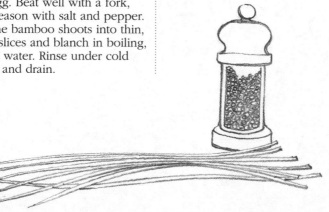

STEAMED PORK WITH GROUND RICE

This spiced pork is dredged in ground rice which makes a deliciously grainy-textured coating. The steaming gives a gentle, moist cooking. Szechuan chilli bean paste is available in specialist food shops and Chinese supermarkets.

Serves 4-6

INGREDIENTS
680g/1½lb pork tenderloin
1 tsp salt
2 tbsps soy sauce
2 tbsps Szechuan chilli bean
  paste
1 tsp sugar
3 slices fresh root ginger, peeled
  and finely shredded
3 shallots, finely chopped
Freshly ground Szechuan pepper
1 tbsp oil
4 tbsps ground rice
1 head of Chinese leaves,
  shredded
Sesame oil to garnish

Cut the pork into bite-sized pieces. Mix together the salt, soy sauce, chilli bean paste, sugar, ginger, shallots, Szechuan pepper and oil. Add the prepared pork and marinate for 20 minutes.

Coat each piece of pork with ground rice and arrange in neat layers on a bed of the shredded cabbage in a steamer. Steam vigorously for 25-30 minutes.

Serve the pork on a bed of the shredded cabbbage leaves. Garnish with sesame oil and more finely chopped shallots or spring onions. Serve with a chilli sauce as a dip if wished.

SHANGHAI LONG-COOKED KNUCKLE OF PORK

Pork knuckles can be bought at bargain prices so it is always good to have a few recipes to hand to make the most of them! The meat will be well cooked after two hours and should just pull off the bone with a spoon and fork.

Serves 4-6

INGREDIENTS

1.4-1.8kg/3-4lb pork hock or knuckle
1.7 litres/3 pints water
3 shallots
150ml/¼ pint soy sauce
60g/2oz sugar
150ml/¼ pint pale dry sherry
4 slices fresh root ginger, peeled
30g/1oz lard

Clean and trim the pork, then slash the meat with a knife to speed cooking. Place in a large, deep pan and cover with the water. Bring to the boil, then simmer for 15 minutes. Discard one third of the water.

Cut the shallots into 2.5cm/1 inch pieces and add them to the pork with the soy sauce, sugar, sherry, ginger and lard. Cover and simmer for 2 hours. Turn the pork over several times during cooking. By the end of the cooking time the water in the pan should have reduced by three quarters. Return to the boil and reduce again by half. The broth or sauce will have become rich and brown.

Serve the pork in a deep bowl with the sauce poured over. Serve with steamed vegetables and rice.

PORK WITH SCRAMBLED EGGS

A very high protein dish to be served with noodles and stir-fried, crispy vegetables. We are more used to scrambled eggs with fish, but meat works well too.

Serves 4

INGREDIENTS
8 eggs
½ onion, finely chopped
1 tbsp oyster sauce
Salt and freshly ground black
    pepper
460g/1lb lean pork
2 tbsps oil
1-2 cloves garlic, chopped
3-4 small Chinese dried black
    mushrooms, soaked for 15
    minutes in warm water
1 tsp sugar
½ tsp soy sauce
200ml/7 fl oz chicken stock
1 tsp cornflour, combined with a
    little water

Beat the eggs together with the onion, oyster sauce and a little pepper. Set aside. Cut the meat into very thin slices. Rinse and drain the mushrooms.

Cook the eggs over a very gentle heat in a frying pan, stirring constantly with a wooden spoon or a spatula until thickened. This should take approximately 10 minutes. Meanwhile, heat the oil in a wok and stir-fry the garlic and the pork. Pour off any excess fat and add the mushrooms, sugar, soy sauce and the stock. Cook until the meat is cooked through. Thicken with the cornflour paste, stirring continuously until the sauce boils and thickens. Place a bed of scrambled eggs on a warm plate and arrange the meat mixture over the eggs.

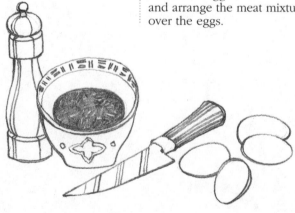

PORK WITH CHINESE VEGETABLES

Add a few fresh mushrooms towards the end of cooking if you like. The sauce for this marinated pork is flavoured with garlic and ginger.

Serves 4

INGREDIENTS
460g/1lb pork fillet or tenderloin
1-2 cloves garlic, chopped
½ tsp chopped fresh root ginger
½ tsp cornflour
Few drops chilli sauce
1 tbsp wine vinegar
1 tbsp soy sauce
225g/8oz bamboo shoots
6-8 Chinese dried black
   mushrooms, soaked for 15
   minutes in warm water
2 tbsps oil
280ml/½ pint chicken stock

Cut the pork into small dice. Add the garlic and ginger, and sprinkle with the cornflour. Add a few drops of chilli sauce, but not too much as it is very hot, then the vinegar. Finally sprinkle with the soy sauce. Leave to marinate for 20 minutes at room temperature.

Cut the bamboo shoots into thin strips, blanch them in boiling, lightly salted water, rinse in cold water and set aside to drain. Rinse the mushrooms and set aside to drain. Remove the meat from the marinade with a slotted spoon and reserve the marinade.

Heat the oil in a wok and stir-fry the meat until tender. Pour off any excess fat and pour in the stock. Stir in first the mushrooms and the bamboo shoots and then the marinade and cook together until boiling and thickened. Serve hot.

STUFFED CHINESE LEAVES

Serve these stuffed cabbage leaves on a bed of special fried rice. Make certain that the Chinese leaves are soft before you fill them, or they will tear instead of rolling up neatly.

Serves 4

INGREDIENTS
225g/8oz lean pork
225g/8oz boneless chicken
120g/4oz Chinese leaves
1 tbsp oil
1-2 cloves garlic, chopped
120g/4oz bean sprouts, blanched
2 tbsps sweetcorn
2 tbsps soy sauce
Salt and freshly ground black
  pepper
420ml/¾ pint duck stock
1 tsp cornflour, combined with a
  little water
Soy sauce to taste

Chop the pork and the chicken finely. Reserve 8 Chinese leaves and shred the remaining leaves finely. Blanch the reserved leaves in boiling water until soft then refresh them in cold water and dry on a tea-towel.

Heat the oil and stir-fry the meat, garlic, shredded Chinese leaves, bean sprouts, sweetcorn, 1 tbsp of the soy sauce, salt and pepper for several minutes. Spread the blanched leaves out and place a small amount of stuffing on each one. Roll up the leaf around the stuffing, beginning at the base and folding in the sides halfway up, to completely enclose the filling. Secure the rolls with wooden cocktail sticks if necessary.

Heat together the stock and the remaining soy sauce. Drop the stuffed rolls into the stock and cook for 5 minutes, turning occasionally. Remove the rolls with a slotted spoon and place them on a heated serving plate. Thicken the sauce by adding the cornflour paste. Heat, stirring continuously, until boiling and thickened. Adjust the seasoning as necessary. To serve, surround the rolls with the sauce, flavoured with a few drops of soy sauce.

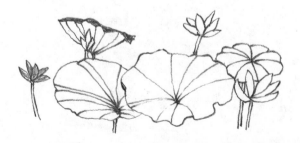

154

PORK WITH BAMBOO SHOOTS

Courgettes and bamboo shoots provide contrasting textures to accompany thin slices of pork. Any left-over courgette flesh may be added to a vegetable stir-fry.

Serves 4

INGREDIENTS
460g/1lb lean pork
Salt and freshly ground black
   pepper
225g/8oz bamboo shoots
1 courgette
2 tbsps oil
1 spring onion, chopped
120ml/4 fl oz chicken stock
1 tbsp soy sauce
1 tsp cornflour, combined with a
   little water

Cut the pork into very thin slices and season with salt and pepper. Cut the bamboo shoots into small squares and blanch in boiling, lightly salted water for 2 minutes. Drain well. Using a sharp knife, peel the courgette thickly lengthways. Discard the remaining flesh and seeds. Slice the peel thinly into strips.

Heat the oil in a wok, add the spring onion and the meat. Stir-fry for 1 minute. Pour off any excess fat and stir in the stock. Add the bamboo shoots and the courgette and cook gently for 6-8 minutes. Stir in the soy sauce and add the cornflour, stirring continuously until the sauce has boiled and thickened. Add salt and pepper to taste. Serve hot.

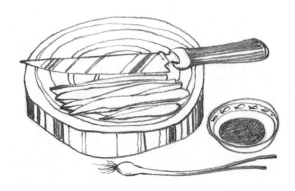

CARAMELISED PORK

Pork fillet, or tenderloin, cooks quickly. I would serve this with egg noodles and stir-fried mushrooms with Chinese leaves.

Serves 4

INGREDIENTS
2 tbsps dark soy sauce
1 tbsp Chinese wine
1 tbsp hoisin sauce
1 tsp honey
Few drops chilli sauce
2 tsps oil
460g/1lb pork fillet
Salt and freshly ground black
    pepper

Preheat an oven to 180°C/350°F/Gas Mark 4. Mix together the soy sauce, wine, hoisin sauce, honey, chilli sauce and the oil. Stir well. Cut any excess fat from the pork fillet and remove any gristle. Tie the fillet up with thin kitchen string to make a neat shape. Place the fillet in an ovenproof dish. Coat with the prepared sauce and cook in the preheated oven for 30 minutes. Baste the roast with the sauce during cooking, so that it builds up in caramelised layers around the meat. Remove the roast from the oven and place the meat on a carving board. Pour any remaining sauce into a sauce boat.

Cut the meat into paper thin slices and arrange on a warmed serving dish. Serve immediately with any remaining sauce.

PORK SPARERIBS WITH CHINESE MUSHROOMS

The sauce for these spareribs is slightly hotter than some as it contains chilli sauce. Add as much as you like.

Serves 4

INGREDIENTS
900g/2lbs pork spareribs
1 carrot, finely sliced
1 leek, finely chopped
1 bay leaf
175g/6oz Chinese dried
 mushrooms, soaked for 15
 minutes in warm water and
 drained
1 tbsp oil
2-3 cloves garlic, chopped
½ tsp chilli sauce
1 tbsp soy sauce
1 tbsp hoisin sauce
1 tsp wine vinegar
280ml/½ pint chicken stock
Salt and freshly ground black
 pepper

Ask your butcher to chop the spareribs into small pieces. Boil plenty of water with the carrot, leek and bay leaf in a large pan. Blanch the spareribs for 1 minute in the boiling water, then drain them well. Cook the mushrooms in the boiling water for 10 minutes, then drain them well too.

Heat the oil in a wok, add the garlic, chilli sauce and the mushrooms. Fry slowly until lightly coloured, then stir in the soy sauce, hoisin sauce, vinegar and stock. Add the spareribs, stirring so that they are well coated in the sauce. Season with salt and pepper to taste and cook, covered, for 10 minutes. Remove the lid and allow the sauce to reduce slightly. Serve piping hot.

PORK WITH GREEN PEPPERS

This simple stir-fry celebrates the fresh flavour of green peppers. The only other vegetables included are for seasoning purposes, so the green peppers really dominate the dish.

Serves 4

INGREDIENTS

460g/1lb pork fillet
2 tbsps oil
1-2 cloves garlic, chopped
2 green peppers, seeded and cut into thin matchsticks
1 tsp wine vinegar
2 tbsps chicken stock
1 tbsp hoisin sauce
Salt and freshly ground black pepper
1 tsp cornflour, combined with a little water

Slice the pork thinly, then cut it into narrow strips. Heat the oil in a wok, add the garlic, green peppers and the meat. Stir well and cook for 1 minute, shaking the wok occasionally. Stir in the vinegar, stock and hoisin sauce. Season to taste with salt and pepper and cook for a further 3 minutes. Stir in the cornflour and cook, stirring continuously, until boiling and thickened. Serve.

STIR-FRIED PORK AND VEGETABLES

Shaohsing wine is rice wine – dry sherry may be used if preferred. The sauce for this pork dish is spicy and very slightly sweet.

Serves 4

Ingredients

1 carrot, cut into thin matchsticks
225g/8oz bean sprouts
2 tbsps oil
1 slice fresh root ginger
1 spring onion, chopped
1-2 cloves garlic, chopped
460g/1lb pork, cut into thin slices
2 tsps Shaohsing wine
280ml/½ pint chicken stock
Salt and freshly ground black
  pepper
½ tsp brown sugar
1 tsp cornflour, combined with a
  little water

Boil a little salted water in a small saucepan. Blanch the carrot strips for 1 minute. Drain well, reserving the water. Wash the bean sprouts under running water then blanch them for 1 minute in the water used for the carrot. Rinse well and drain.

Heat the oil in a wok. Stir-fry the ginger, spring onion and garlic until slightly coloured, then add the meat, stir well and cook for 1 minute. Add the well-drained vegetables, sake and stock. Season with salt and pepper, and stir-fry for 2 minutes. Using a slotted spoon, remove the meat and vegetables, and keep warm. Add the sugar to the contents of the wok and thicken the sauce with the cornflour paste, stirring until boiling and thickened. Remove the ginger, return the meat and vegetables to the wok and serve hot.

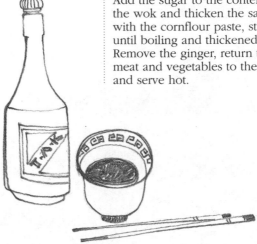

LION'S HEAD

*This recipe title describes the meat balls sitting on a 'mane'
of cabbage! Use Chinese cabbage, pak choi or Chinese leaves
but do not shred them or they will overcook. Serve as part of
a mixed buffet meal.*

Serves 6

INGREDIENTS
900g/2lbs minced pork
2 shallots, finely chopped
2 slices fresh root ginger, peeled
    and finely chopped
2 tbsps pale dry sherry
2 tbsps cornflour
1 tsp salt
30g/1oz lard
460g/1lb Chinese cabbage or
    Chinese leaves, quartered
    lengthways
280ml/½ pint chicken stock

Mix together the pork, shallots,
ginger, sherry, cornflour, and half
the salt. Shape the mixture into
six meatballs. Melt the lard in a
deep pan, add the cabbage and
remaining salt, and fry for 30
seconds. Place the meatballs on
the cabbage and pour the stock
over the top. Bring to the boil,
then cover the pan tightly.
Simmer gently for 30-40 minutes.
Serve hot. (Alternatively the
meatballs may be fried in a little
lard, with soy sauce and sugar,
before placing them on top of
the cabbage).

PORK SLICES WITH CRUNCHY VEGETABLES

This is a very light, summery dish; steamed pork with crispy steamed vegetables served with a fragrant, cold sauce.

Serves 4

INGREDIENTS
1 tbsp light soy sauce
1 tbsp Chinese wine
1 tsp sugar
2.5cm/1 inch piece of fresh root ginger, peeled and finely chopped
460g/1lb lean pork
Salt and freshly ground black pepper
1 carrot
1 stick celery
½ bulb fennel

Make the sauce; mix together the soy sauce, Chinese wine, sugar and ginger in a small bowl. Allow to stand for 30 minutes for the flavours to blend before serving.

Cut the pork into very thin slices and season with salt and pepper. Cut the carrot, celery and fennel into thin julienne strips. Place the vegetables in a steaming basket and steam for 3 minutes. Remove the basket from the steamer and lay the slices of pork over the vegetables. Return the basket to the steamer and cook for another 5 minutes. Serve the steamed pork and vegetables accompanied by the cold sauce.

BRAISED PORK WITH SPINACH & MUSHROOMS

*Spinach and nutmeg are used together in many
international cuisines. You might think that such a
delicate flavour would get lost in this dish, but not at all –
try it and see.*

Serves 4

INGREDIENTS
4 Chinese dried mushrooms
2 tbsps peanut oil
½ tsp ground nutmeg
225g/8oz spinach leaves,
    washed, stalks removed, and
    shredded
1 clove garlic, crushed
1 onion, quartered
1 tbsp flour
Salt and freshly ground black
    pepper
460g/1lb pork tenderloin, cut
    into thin strips
2 tbsps water

Soak the mushrooms in hot water for 20 minutes, then drain. Discard the stems, slice the caps finely and set aside. Heat a wok, add 1 tsp of the oil and roll it around to coat the surface of the wok. Add the nutmeg and spinach and cook gently for 5 minutes, then remove the spinach from the pan. Add the remaining oil to the wok and fry the garlic and onion over a gentle heat for 5 minutes. Remove from the wok.

Meanwhile, season the flour with salt and pepper and use it to coat the pork. Fry the pork in the wok until each piece is browned all over. Add the water and mushrooms, and return the onion mixture to the wok. Cover and simmer gently for 10 minutes, stirring occasionally. Add the spinach and season to taste, then cook, uncovered, for 2 minutes. Serve hot with steamed rice.

PORK WITH CHILLI

Always take great care to remove the seeds from peppers and chillies – that's where the real heat is hidden! Slice or chop chillies very finely and rinse your hands after preparation to remove all the strong juices.

Serves 4

INGREDIENTS
1 clove garlic, crushed
1 tsp sugar
1 tsp peanut oil
1 tsp Chinese wine or dry sherry
1 tsp cornflour
275g/10oz lean pork fillet, cut into 2.5cm/1 inch slices
150ml/¼ pint peanut oil, for deep-frying
1 green pepper, seeded and sliced
1 red chilli, seeded and finely sliced
4 spring onions, chopped

Sauce
1 tsp chilli powder
2 tbsps dark soy sauce
1 tsp Worcestershire sauce
½ tsp five-spice powder
Pinch of salt

Mix together the garlic, sugar, 1 tsp peanut oil, wine and cornflour, and pour the mixture over the prepared pork. Cover and leave for at least 1 hour, stirring occasionally. Meanwhile, combine the ingredients for the sauce in a bowl, mix well and set aside.

Heat the oil for deep-frying in a wok until hot. Add the pork and fry until golden brown and cooked through – about 10 minutes. Remove the pork with a slotted spoon, drain on absorbent kitchen paper and set aside. Carefully remove all but 1 tbsp of oil from the wok. Heat and add the green pepper, chilli and spring onions. Stir-fry for 2 minutes. Add the prepared sauce and fried pork, and bring to the boil, stirring continuously. Adjust the seasoning. Serve immediately with rice or noodles.

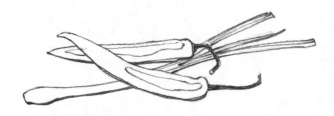

SWEET & SOUR PORK

Serves 2-4

INGREDIENTS

225g/8oz pork fillet, cut into
  1.25cm/½ inch cubes
Oil for deep-frying
1 onion, sliced
1 green pepper, seeded and
  sliced
225g/8oz can pineapple chunks,
  juice reserved

Batter
120g/4oz plain flour
4 tbsps cornflour
1½ tsps baking powder
Pinch of salt
1 tbsp oil
Water

Sweet & Sour Sauce
2 tbsps cornflour
120g/4oz light brown sugar
Pinch of salt
120ml/4 fl oz cider vinegar or
  rice vinegar
1 clove garlic, crushed
1 tsp fresh root ginger, peeled
  and grated
6 tbsps tomato ketchup
6 tbsps reserved pineapple juice

First prepare the batter. Sift the flour, cornflour, baking powder and salt into a bowl. Make a well in the centre and add the oil and enough water to make a thick, smooth batter. Using a wooden spoon, stir the ingredients, gradually incorporating the flour, and beat until smooth.

Heat enough oil in a wok to deep-fry the pork. Dip the pork cubes one at a time into the batter and drop into the hot oil – chopsticks are ideal for doing this. Fry 4-5 pieces of pork at a time and remove them with a slotted spoon and drain on absorbent kitchen paper. Continue frying until all the pork is cooked.

Drain most of the oil from the wok and add the sliced onion, pepper and pineapple. Cook over a high heat for 1-2 minutes, then remove the vegetables and pineapple and set aside. Mix all the sauce ingredients together and pour into the wok. Bring slowly to the boil, stirring continuously until thickened. Allow to simmer for about 1-2 minutes or until completely clear. Add the vegetables, pineapple and pork cubes to the sauce and stir to coat the pork completely. Reheat for 1-2 minutes and serve immediately.

PORK WITH BLACK BEAN SAUCE

Making your own black bean sauce for this stir-fry gives a much stronger and punchier flavour. The sauce also goes well with chicken and beef.

Serves 4

INGREDIENTS
Sauce
225g/8oz lean pork, cut into
  2.5cm/1 inch cubes
1 tbsp oil
1 red pepper, seeded and sliced

3 tbsps black beans, rinsed in
  cold water and crushed with
  the back of a spoon
2 tbsps Chinese wine, or dry
  sherry
1 tsp grated fresh root ginger
2 tbsps light soy sauce
3 cloves garlic, crushed
1 tbsp cornflour
150ml/¼ pint water

Prepare the sauce. Mix together the black beans, wine, ginger, soy sauce and garlic. Blend the cornflour with 2 tbsps of the water and add it to the mixture. Place the pork in a bowl and cover with the sauce. Leave to marinate for at least 30 minutes.

Heat a wok, add the oil and stir-fry the red pepper strips for 3 minutes. Remove and set aside. Add the pork, reserving the marinade sauce, and stir-fry until browned all over. Add the marinade and remaining water, then bring to the boil. Reduce the heat, cover the wok and simmer for about 30 minutes, until the pork is tender, stirring occasionally. Add more water during cooking if necessary. Just before serving, add the red pepper and heat through. Serve with plain boiled rice.

PORK WITH PLUM SAUCE

Plum sauce is deep red in colour, spicy in flavour and a vital part of Chinese cookery. It is often served with crispy duck in pancakes. Most supermarkets sell it in bottles and you will certainly get it in Chinese grocers and delicatessens.

Serves 4

INGREDIENTS
1 tbsp cornflour
1 tsp sesame oil
1 tbsp light soy sauce
1 tbsp sherry
1 tbsp brown sugar
½ tsp cinnamon
Pinch of salt
460g/1lb lean pork fillet, cut into
   2.5cm/1 inch cubes
2 tbsps peanut oil
1 spring onion, finely sliced
1 clove garlic, crushed
4 tbsps prepared plum sauce
4 tbsps water
Freshly ground black pepper
Spring onion flowers (see recipe
   for Barbecued Spareribs)

Mix together the cornflour, sesame oil, light soy sauce, sherry, brown sugar, cinnamon and salt. Pour the marinade over the pork in a bowl, toss together and leave to stand for a few minutes. Remove the pork and reserve the marinade.

Heat a wok and add the peanut oil. Add the pork, and stir-fry until golden brown all over. Stir in the spring onion, garlic, plum sauce and water, and mix together well. Bring to the boil, cover and simmer gently for 15 minutes, or until the pork is tender, stirring occasionally. Add the reserved marinade from the pork, and bring to the boil. Simmer gently for a further 5 minutes. Garnish with spring onion flowers. Serve hot with boiled rice.

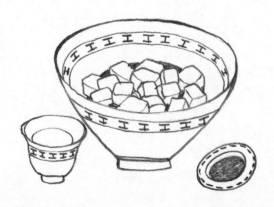

FIVE-SPICE BEEF WITH BROCCOLI

This is such an easy recipe to prepare. The rich green of the broccoli looks wonderful against the brown of the spiced beef, garnished with long lengths of chives.

Serves 4

INGREDIENTS
225g/8oz fillet or rump steak
1 clove garlic, crushed
½ tsp finely grated fresh root ginger
½ tsp five-spice powder
2 tbsps peanut oil
120g/4oz broccoli florets
1 tbsp dark soy sauce
½ tsp salt
150ml/¼ pint hot water
2 tsps cornflour
1 tbsp cold water
Bunch of chives, snipped into 2.5cm/1 inch lengths

Cut the steak into thin slices, then into narrow strips and mix together with the garlic, ginger and five-spice powder.

Heat a wok, add 1 tbsp of the oil and stir-fry the broccoli for 8 minutes. Remove the broccoli and add the remaining oil to the wok. Add the beef and seasonings and stir-fry for 3 minutes. Stir in the broccoli, the soy sauce, salt and hot water, and heat to simmering point.

Blend the cornflour and cold water, pour into the wok and cook, stirring continuously, until boiling and thickened. Toss in the chives, stir, and serve immediately with boiled rice.

STIR-FRIED BEEF WITH OYSTER SAUCE

Stir-fried Beef with Oyster Sauce has a deep intensity of flavours with peppery overtones. Serve it with fried rice and mixed Chinese vegetables.

Serves 4

INGREDIENTS
340g/12oz lean beef
175g/6oz broccoli
280ml/½ pint oil for deep-frying
2 tbsps oyster sauce
½ tsp salt
1 tsp sugar
2 spring onions, chopped

Marinade
2 tsps white wine
1 tbsp soy sauce
½ tsp salt
1 tsp sugar
¼ tsp baking powder
¼ tsp freshly ground black
   pepper
1 tbsp water
2 tsps cornflour
2 tbsps oil

Cut the beef into thin slices. Mix all the marinade ingredients together, add the beef and leave for several hours. Remove the beef with a slotted spoon and discard the marinade. Cook the broccoli, broken into florets, in boiling salted water for 15-20 minutes, then drain.

Heat the oil in a wok, then deep-fry the marinated beef for 20 seconds. Remove the beef with a slotted spoon. Remove all but 4 tbsps of oil from the wok. Stir-fry the broccoli in the remaining oil for 30 seconds, then add the beef, sprinkle with oyster sauce, salt, sugar and chopped spring onions. Stir-fry for a further 30 seconds, then serve.

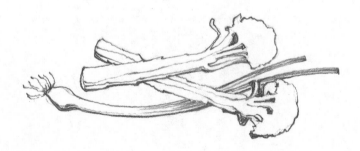

SHREDDED BEEF WITH VEGETABLES

The beef used in stir-fries cooks very quickly so it has to be of top quality to ensure that it will be tender. Fillet or rump steaks give the best results.

Serves 4

INGREDIENTS

225g/8oz lean fillet or rump steak, cut into thin strips
½ tsp salt
4 tbsps vegetable oil
1 red and 1 green chilli, cut in half, seeded and cut into strips
1 tsp vinegar
1 stick celery, cut into thin 5cm/2 inch strips
2 carrots, cut into thin 5cm/2 inch strips
1 leek, white part only, sliced into thin 5cm/2 inch strips
2 cloves garlic, finely chopped
1 tsp light soy sauce
1 tsp dark soy sauce
2 tsps Chinese wine or dry sherry
1 tsp caster sugar
½ tsp freshly ground black pepper

Place the strips of beef in a large bowl and sprinkle with the salt. Rub the salt into the meat and leave to stand for 5 minutes. Heat 1 tbsp of the oil in a large wok. When the oil begins to smoke, reduce the heat and stir in the beef and the chillies. Stir-fry for 4-5 minutes. Add the remaining oil and continue stir-frying the beef until it becomes crispy. Add the vinegar and stir until it evaporates, then add the celery, carrots, leek and garlic. Stir-fry for 2 minutes.

Mix together the soy sauces, wine or sherry, sugar and ground pepper. Pour the mixture over the beef and cook for 2 minutes. Serve immediately.

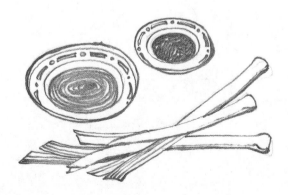

BEEF WITH ONIONS

Beef fillet is such a treat! It cooks very quickly and is always very tender. As we might serve fried steak and onions, so this dish uses lots of onions to flavour the meat.

Serves 4

INGREDIENTS
460g/1lb fillet of beef

Marinade
1 tbsp oil
1 tsp sesame oil
1 tbsp Chinese wine
1 tbsp oil
2.5cm/1 inch piece fresh root ginger, peeled and roughly chopped
3 onions, finely sliced
1 clove garlic, chopped
280ml/½ pint beef stock
Pinch of sugar
2 tbsps dark soy sauce
1 tsp cornflour, combined with a little water
Salt and freshly ground black pepper

Cut the beef fillet into very thin slices. Mix together the marinade ingredients and stir in the meat. Leave for 30 minutes.

Heat 1 tbsp oil in a wok and stir-fry the ginger, onions and garlic until lightly browned. Lift the meat out of the marinade with a slotted spoon and discard the marinade. Add the meat to the wok and stir-fry with the vegetables. Add the stock, sugar and soy sauce and cook for 4 minutes. Thicken the sauce with the cornflour mixture, stirring continuously until boiling and thickened. Season with salt and pepper and serve immediately.

MA PO TOU FU

The addition of bean curd or tofu to this recipe makes a little minced beef go a long way! The beef, even such a small amount, gives flavour and texture to the hot and spicy sauce.

Serves 4

INGREDIENTS
460g/1lb tofu or bean curd
2 tbsps salted black beans
3 spring onions
3 cloves garlic
4 chillies, seeded
3 tbsps oil
120g/4oz minced beef
1 tsp salt
225ml/8 fl oz stock
1 tbsp cornflour
1 tbsp soy sauce
½ tsp freshly ground black
   pepper

Simmer the whole cakes of bean curd or tofu in water for 3 minutes, then drain them and cut into bite-sized pieces. Soak the black beans in water for 20 minutes. Chop the spring onions, garlic and chillies. Drain the black beans.

Heat the oil in a large wok, add the beef, salt and black beans and stir-fry for 3-4 minutes. Add the chillies, spring onions and garlic and cook for a further 2 minutes before adding half the stock and the tofu. Simmer for 4 minutes.

Mix the cornflour with the remaining stock and soy sauce. Pour the mixture into the wok, bring to the boil and simmer for 2-3 minutes. Sprinkle with the black pepper and serve with rice.

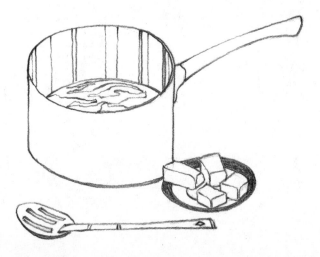

FILLET STEAK, CHINESE-STYLE

A little meat goes a long way in this recipe – in many western countries it would be quite usual for one person to eat 8oz of steak by themselves. Adding vegetables helps to make the meat go further.

Serves 4

INGREDIENTS

225g/8oz fillet or rump steak, cut into 2.5cm/1 inch pieces
Pinch of bicarbonate of soda
1 tsp light soy sauce
1 tsp sesame oil
1 tsp Chinese wine, or 2 tsps dry sherry
2 tsps sugar
1 tsp cornflour
Salt and freshly ground black pepper
2 tbsps dark soy sauce
4 tbsps water
3 tbsps peanut oil
2 cloves garlic, crushed
2 spring onions, sliced diagonally into 1.25cm/½ inch pieces
½ tsp crushed fresh root ginger
425g/15oz can straw mushrooms, drained
425g/15oz can baby sweetcorn, drained
1 tbsp oyster sauce
Spring onion flowers (see recipe for Barbecued Spareribs), to garnish

Place the steak in a bowl and sprinkle with the bicarbonate of soda. Mix together the light soy sauce, sesame oil, wine, half the sugar, half the cornflour, and seasoning. Pour over the steak and leave for at least an hour, turning the meat occasionally in the marinade.

Meanwhile, make a sauce by mixing 2 tbsps of dark soy sauce, the remaining sugar and cornflour, and the water. Mix together and set aside.

Heat a wok, add the peanut oil and, when hot, fry the steak for 4 minutes. Remove the steak with a slotted spoon and set aside. Stir-fry the garlic, spring onions, ginger, mushrooms and baby sweetcorn briefly then add the steak and oyster sauce and mix well. Add the sauce mixture and bring to the boil. Cook for 3 minutes, stirring occasionally. Serve hot with rice, garnished with spring onion flowers.

STIR-FRIED BEEF WITH MANGO SLICES

I have served this dish cold in buffets several times and it has always been a great success. However, it is more usual to serve it hot, with thread egg noodles or boiled rice.

Serves 4

INGREDIENTS
225g/8oz fillet of beef
1 large mango
4 tbsps oil
1 tbsp shredded fresh root ginger
1 shallot, finely sliced

Marinade
1 tbsp white wine
1 tbsp soy sauce
1 tsp cornflour
¼ tsp sugar
¼ tsp freshly ground black
  pepper

Cut the beef into thin bite-sized pieces. Blend together the ingredients for the marinade, add the beef and leave for 20 minutes. Peel and slice the mango.

Set a wok over a high heat, add the oil and wait until almost smoking. Reduce the heat to a moderate setting, add the beef and ginger and stir-fry for 1-2 minutes. Remove the beef and ginger with a slotted spoon. Toss the mango slices in the hot oil for a few seconds, return the beef and ginger to the wok, and add the shallot. Stir-fry for a further few seconds, then serve immediately.

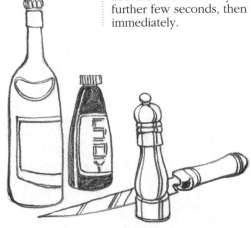

BEEF WITH TOMATO & PEPPER IN BLACK BEAN SAUCE

No extra salt is needed to season this dish as the black beans are very salty and savoury. Marinate the beef in the soy sauce for at least 10 minutes.

Serves 6

INGREDIENTS

2 large tomatoes
2 tbsps salted black beans
2 tbsps water
4 tbsps dark soy sauce
1 tbsp cornflour
1 tbsp dry sherry
1 tsp sugar
460g/1lb rump steak, cut into
  thin strips
1 small green pepper, seeded
4 tbsps oil
175ml/6 fl oz beef stock
Pinch of freshly ground black
  pepper

Core the tomatoes and cut them into 16 wedges. Crush the black beans, add the water and set aside. Combine the soy sauce, cornflour, sherry and sugar in a bowl. Cut the meat into thin strips, add to the marinade and set aside. Cut the pepper into 1.25cm/½ inch diagonal pieces.

Heat a wok and add the oil. When hot, stir-fry the green pepper pieces for about 1 minute then remove them with a slotted spoon. Add the meat and the soy sauce mixture to the wok and stir-fry for about 2 minutes. Add the soaked black beans and the stock. Bring to the boil and allow to thicken slightly. Return the peppers to the wok and add the tomatoes and pepper to taste. Heat through for 1 minute and serve immediately.

174

BEEF WITH CHINESE MUSHROOMS

This Chinese recipe is most unusual as the meat is dry-fried, rather than being cooked in a sauce. It makes a very pleasant change.

Serves 4

INGREDIENTS

1 tsp cornflour
1 tbsp light soy sauce
1 egg white
1 tsp sugar
460g/1lb rump steak, thinly sliced
6 Chinese dried black mushrooms, soaked for 1 hour in warm water
2 tbsps oil
1-2 cloves garlic, chopped
Salt and freshly ground black pepper
2 tbsps Chinese wine

Place the cornflour in a small bowl and stir in the soy sauce. Beat in the egg white and the sugar, mixing thoroughly to combine all the ingredients. Add the slices of beef and leave to marinate for 1 hour. Drain the mushrooms, which should be very soft, and cut them into thin strips.

Heat the oil in a wok, stir-fry the garlic, the beef in its marinade and the mushrooms for 4-5 minutes and season with salt and pepper. Stir in the wine and serve as soon as it has evaporated.

SZECHUAN MEATBALLS

Szechuan Province lends its name to many classic Chinese dishes, all of which are highly spiced. Ginger, usually the fresh root variety, is one of the commonest ingredients in this vibrant style of cookery.

Serves 4

INGREDIENTS

90g/3oz blanched almonds
460g/1lb minced beef
1 tsp grated fresh root ginger
1 clove garlic, crushed
½ large green pepper, seeded and chopped
Dash Szechuan, chilli, or Tabasco sauce
5 tbsps soy sauce
Oil for frying
120ml/4 fl oz vegetable stock
1 tbsp rice wine or white wine vinegar
2 tsps honey
1 tbsp sherry
1 tbsp cornflour
4 spring onions, sliced diagonally

Spread the almonds evenly in a grill pan, and grill under a low heat for 3-4 minutes, or until lightly toasted. Stir the almonds often to prevent them from burning. Roughly chop the almonds using a large sharp knife, then place them in a large bowl. Add the meat, ginger, garlic, green pepper, Szechuan sauce, and 2 tbsps of the soy sauce. Using a wooden spoon, or your hands, mix well to ensure that the ingredients are well blended, then divide the mixture into 16 and roll each piece into a small meatball on a lightly floured board.

Heat a little oil in a large frying pan and add about half the meatballs in a single layer. Cook over a low heat for about 20 minutes, turning the meatballs frequently until they are well browned all over. Transfer them to a serving dish and keep warm while cooking the remaining meatballs. Set aside as before.

Stir the remaining 3 tbsps of soy sauce, stock and vinegar into the frying pan and bring to the boil. Boil briskly for about 30 seconds, then add the honey and stir until dissolved. Blend the sherry and cornflour together in a small bowl, and add the paste to the hot sauce. Cook, stirring all the time, until boiling and thickened. Arrange the meatballs on a serving dish and sprinkle with the sliced spring onions. Pour the sauce over, and serve immediately.

BEEF WITH GINGER SAUCE

*Another very quick dish, both to prepare and to cook.
Chopped tomatoes give an extra richness of colour to the
ginger sauce.*

Serves 4

INGREDIENTS
460g/1lb fillet of beef
2 tbsps oil
2 tbsps fresh root ginger, peeled
  and cut into small matchsticks
2 tomatoes, skinned, seeded and
  finely chopped
1 tsp sugar
1 tbsp red wine vinegar
2 tbsps soy sauce
Salt and freshly ground black
  pepper

Cut the beef into very thin slices. Heat the oil in a wok, add the meat and the ginger and stir-fry for 1 minute. Pour off any excess fat, and stir in the tomato. Reduce the heat and add the sugar, vinegar and the soy sauce. Cook for a few minutes to allow the flavours to develop, then season with salt and pepper to taste and serve immediately.

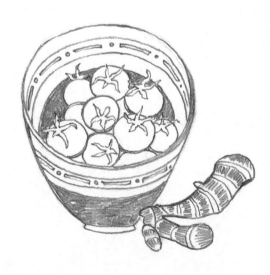

STEAK WITH BLACK BEAN SAUCE

Black beans are used widely in Chinese cooking. They are soy beans and are fermented in salt, producing a strong, savoury flavour. Use them sparingly in meat and vegetable dishes. They are available canned in specialist food shops.

Serves 4

INGREDIENTS

225g/8oz fillet or rump steak, thinly sliced
Pinch of bicarbonate of soda
3 tbsps light soy sauce
3 tsps sugar
1 tsp Chinese wine, or 2 tsps dry sherry
1 tsp sesame oil
Salt and freshly ground black pepper
4 tbsps peanut oil
3 cloves garlic, crushed
1 tsp grated fresh root ginger
1 large onion, chopped
1 large green pepper, seeded and diced
227g/8oz can bamboo shoots, drained
3 tsps black beans
1 tbsp cornflour

Place the sliced steak in a bowl, and sprinkle it with the bicarbonate of soda. Add 1 tbsp of the light soy sauce, 1 tsp of the sugar, the wine, sesame oil, salt and pepper, and leave to marinate for at least 1 hour.

Heat a wok and add 2 tbsps of the peanut oil. When hot, add the steak and the marinade and fry quickly. Remove the wok from the heat, remove the steak and juices, and set aside. Make a black bean sauce by crushing the beans and mixing with the garlic, ginger, 1 tsp of the sugar and 1 tbsp of the peanut oil.

Heat the wok, add the remaining oil and pour in the black bean mixture. Return the steak to the wok and add the onion, pepper and bamboo shoots, then mix well. Make a seasoning sauce by mixing the cornflour with the remaining 2 tbsps of light soy sauce and 1 tsp sugar. When well mixed, pour into the wok and stir. Bring to the boil and cook for 3 minutes. Serve hot with rice.

PEKING BEEF

Cold beef, served thinly sliced after marinating or cooking in a spiced liquor, is a popular dish around the world. This version could be prepared in a heavy pan or an earthenware casserole, but a covered wok is the traditional cooking utensil.

Serves 8

INGREDIENTS
900g/2lb joint topside of beef
420ml/¾ pint white wine
570ml/1 pint water
2 whole spring onions, roots trimmed
2.5cm/1 inch piece fresh root ginger
3 pieces star anise
150ml/¼ pint soy sauce
2 tsps sugar
1 carrot
2 sticks celery
Half a mooli (daikon) radish

Place the beef in a wok and add the white wine, water, spring onions, ginger and star anise. Cover and simmer for about 1 hour. Add the soy sauce and sugar, stir and simmer for a further 30 minutes, or until the beef is tender. Allow the beef to cool in the liquid.

Shred all the remaining vegetables finely. Blanch them in boiling water for about 1 minute. Rinse under cold water, drain and leave to dry. When the meat is cold, remove it from the liquid and cut into thin slices. Arrange on a serving plate and strain the liquid over it. Scatter the shredded vegetables over the beef and serve cold.

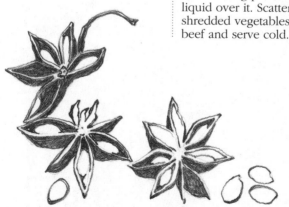

179

BEEF WITH PINEAPPLE & PEPPERS

*All Chinese dishes have such fragrant and descriptive names.
This recipe is sweet and fruity with rich and strongly
contrasting flavours. Serve with plain boiled rice or noodles.*

Serves 4

INGREDIENTS
2 tbsps light soy sauce
1 tsp sugar
2 tsps cornflour
2 tbsps water
460g/1lb fillet or rump steak,
  thinly sliced
1 tbsp peanut oil
1 tsp chopped fresh root ginger
2 cloves garlic, crushed
1 onion, roughly chopped
1 green pepper, seeded and
  chopped
1 red pepper, seeded and
  chopped
227g/8oz can pineapple slices,
  drained and chopped

Sauce
1 tbsp plum sauce
1 tbsp dark soy sauce
1 tsp sugar
1 tsp sesame oil
1 tsp cornflour
4 tbsps water
Salt and freshly ground black
  pepper

Combine the light soy sauce with
the sugar and cornflour and 2
tbsps of water and pour over the
thinly sliced steak. Toss well,
then set aside for at least 30
minutes, turning occasionally.

Heat a wok and add the peanut
oil. Add the ginger, garlic, onion
and peppers, and stir-fry for 3
minutes. Remove the vegetables
from the wok and set aside. Add
extra oil if necessary and stir-fry
the beef for 2 minutes, separating
the pieces. Remove the beef from
the wok and add it to the
vegetables. Mix together all the
sauce ingredients in the wok and
heat until the sauce boils and
begins to thicken. Return the
vegetables and the beef to the
wok, adding the pineapple, and
toss together over a high heat
until heated through. Serve with
boiled rice.

STIR-FRIED LAMB WITH SESAME SEEDS

Lamb is not used as widely as pork and beef in Chinese cookery. This recipe is unusual as the lightly caramelised lamb is sprinkled with sesame seeds before serving. A half shoulder of lamb should give sufficient meat for the dish.

Serves 4

INGREDIENTS
570g/1¼lbs shoulder of lamb, boned
2 tbsps oil
2 onions, thinly sliced
½ clove garlic, chopped
120ml/4 fl oz lamb stock or other meat stock
1 tsp sugar
1 tbsp soy sauce
½ tsp wine vinegar
Salt and freshly ground black pepper
1 tbsp sesame seeds

Cut away any excess fat from the lamb and slice the meat very thinly. Heat the oil in a wok and stir-fry the lamb. Remove when cooked and set aside. Fry the onions and garlic in the same oil until transparent, then remove them and set aside. Pour off any excess fat and put the meat back in the wok with the lamb stock, sugar, soy sauce and vinegar. Continue cooking until the sauce is reduced. Season to taste with salt and pepper. When the meat is lightly caramelized, sprinkle it with the sesame seeds and stir until the meat is evenly coated. Serve hot on a bed of the onions.

LAMB WITH TRANSPARENT NOODLES

Transparent noodles are available in most large supermarkets and specialist food shops. They are quick to prepare and interesting to eat!

Serves 4

INGREDIENTS

460g/1lb lean boneless lamb
120g/4oz transparent noodles
2 tbsps oil
2-3 cloves garlic, chopped
1 spring onion, chopped
2 tbsps soy sauce
200ml/7 fl oz lamb stock
Salt and freshly ground brlack pepper

Cut the meat into thin slices. Bring a large quantity of salted water to the boil, add the noodles and cook them for just 45 seconds. Rinse immediately in cold water and set aside to drain.

Heat the oil in a wok and stir-fry the garlic and spring onion. Add the meat slices and stir-fry for 1 minute. Stir in the soy sauce and the stock and cook over a gentle heat until the meat is cooked through and tender. Add the well-drained noodles and allow to heat through. Adjust the seasoning, adding salt and pepper as necessary. Serve hot.

LAMBS' KIDNEYS
WITH ASPARAGUS

*I love kidneys and asparagus is one of my favourite
vegetables, so this recipe might have been created for me! The
sauce is sweet and spicy and the overall flavour of the dish is
excellent.*

Serves 4

INGREDIENTS
12 green asparagus spears
4 lambs' kidneys
Salt and freshly ground black
  pepper
120g/4oz small black Chinese
  dried mushrooms, soaked for
  15 minutes in warm water
2 tbsps oil
1 shallot, chopped
1 tsp dark soy sauce
1 tbsp hoisin sauce
200ml/7 fl oz chicken stock
Few drops chilli sauce

Peel and trim the asparagus and
cook in boiling, lightly salted
water until tender. Rinse in cold
water and set aside to drain. Cut
the kidneys in half, cutting out
any tubes and gristle. Season
with salt and pepper. Cook the

mushrooms for about 10 minutes
in a small quantity of boiling
water. Rinse them in cold water
and set aside to drain.

Heat the oil in a wok and cook
the kidneys for approximately 3
minutes. Remove them and place
on absorbent kitchen paper to
remove any blood. Pour off any
excess fat from the wok and add
the shallot, soy sauce, hoisin
sauce, mushrooms, stock and
chilli sauce. Cook for 2 minutes.
Return the kidneys to the wok
and cook until the sauce is
slightly reduced. Adjust the
seasoning, adding salt and
pepper to taste. Reheat the
asparagus by steaming lightly.
Serve hot, with the kidneys in
their sauce.

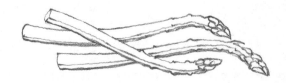

VEGETABLES

The tradition of vegetarian cuisine is rooted in the ancient Bhuddist monasteries of China, and the influence of their wonderfully fragrant and varied cooking is clearly seen in many of the vegetable dishes that are enjoyed throughout China.

Stir-frying for Crisp, Flavoursome Results

Both steaming and cooking in a hot, sweet sauce or gravy gives lightly cooked vegetables which retain a surprising degree of crispness. However, it is the popular and most widely used method of Chinese cooking, stir-frying, that is the ideal way to produce the crisp, crunchy vegetables that are so much a part of Chinese cooking.

The advantages of stir-frying are numerous: it's quick, it retains the bright colours of the vegetables, leading to attractive presentation, and it retains many of the vitamins and minerals that are lost when vegetables are boiled. Vitamin C is found in many vegetables and is water-soluble and therefore destroyed by boiling in water, so stir-frying is a good cooking method for vegetables.

It's Knowing When to Stop!

Well, you might say that about many of the hazards and pitfalls of life, but in this instance I am merely offering a gentle culinary suggestion that will ensure successful vegetable cookery! So many vegetable dishes are absolutely ruined because they are overcooked, leaving a lifeless mush of colourless, watery remains. I always think that the cooking of vegetables is one of the most difficult things about entertaining at home, if you want to appear relaxed and able to sit down with your guests. With Chinese cookery, and especially with stir-frying, it is easy to produce one or two dishes of vegetables in just a few minutes before your guests come to the table.

Very few vegetables are eaten raw in China and even salads are comprised of vegetables that have been lightly cooked. Our recipe for Chinese Leaf Salad with Mushrooms is a typical example of a salad served hot, with the vegetables stir-fried, whilst the Bean Sprout Salad recipe has the bean sprouts cooked and then chilled with the other vegetables before serving.

An Ever-changing Cuisine

No truly great traditions remain unchanged if they are to stay healthy and Chinese cookery, like that of the French, is constantly adapting its great dishes of centuries past to include new cooking techniques and foods that have recently arrived from foreign shores.

China is such a diverse and ancient civilisation that it is almost impossible to believe that they haven't had everything available in some part of the country for ever! This is not so, and many vegetables, such as tomatoes and sweet potatoes have only been introduced to Chinese cookery relatively recently. When you consider the amount of carrots that are found in Chinese restaurants, and the glorious carrot sculptures

that are so often centrepieces of Chinese buffets, it is incredible to realise that carrots, too, are a relatively new introduction to the Chinese diet.

Special Vegetables for a Special Cuisine

The Chinese use many vegetables which are common to cuisines around the world but they also have special varieties which truly make an oriental dish. Many of these are available canned throughout the world but, of course, when at all possible, fresh is best.

Bean Sprouts are usually sprouted mung beans. They are crunchy in texture and should be used on the day of purchase – they never seem to keep very well, even in the refrigerator. They are generally stir-fried for a very short time, but may be cooked for longer in a dish that is served with a gravy-like sauce. Canned bean sprouts are, in my opinion, the least successful of all 'convenience' oriental vegetables and are totally lacking in texture.

Bamboo Shoots are only really available fresh in the Far East. Elsewhere they are cooked and canned – I find these most acceptable, but I have never been lucky enough to have the fresh shoots. They are cut when about 6 inches high, then stripped of their outer layers and cooked. The roots are conical in shape and slices are taken from them, producing the strips of bamboo shoot with which we are all familiar.

There are several varieties of *Water Chestnuts* but the most commonly used one is a tuber which is cultivated in China, Japan and the East Indies. We find these canned in our shops and supermarkets and they retain their crunchy texture well. Water chestnuts are usually sliced before being added to numerous Chinese dishes.

STIR-FRIED CHINESE LEAVES

A very simple vegetable dish, yet with plenty of flavour and fire from the chilli.

Serves 4

INGREDIENTS
460g/1lb Chinese leaves
2 courgettes
2 tbsps oil
2-3 cloves garlic, chopped
1 red chilli, seeded and finely chopped
1 tbsp soy sauce
Salt and freshly ground black pepper
Few drops sesame oil

Shred the Chinese leaves quite finely. Prepare the courgettes, first topping and tailing them and then cutting them into matchsticks. Heat the oil in a wok, add the Chinese leaves and garlic and stir-fry for 2 minutes. Add the courgettes, chilli, soy sauce, salt and pepper. Continue cooking for 3 minutes then serve hot with the sesame oil drizzled on top.

VEGETABLE CHOP SUEY

Use a good variety of vegetables, all cut into even-sized pieces, for this classic dish. It is served with plenty of richly flavoured sauce.

Serves 4

INGREDIENTS
1 green pepper, seeded
1 red pepper, seeded
1 carrot
½ cucumber
1 courgette, thickly peeled, centre discarded
1 onion
2 cloves garlic, sliced
2 tbsps oil
2 tsps sugar
2 tbsps soy sauce
120ml/4 fl oz chicken stock
Salt and freshly ground black pepper

Cut all the vegetables into thin slices. Prepare the onion by slicing it in half, then into quarters, and finally into thin, even slices. Chop the garlic very finely.

Heat the oil in a wok and stir-fry the peppers and garlic for 30 seconds. Add the onion and carrot and stir-fry for a further 30 seconds, then add the cucumber and the courgette and cook for a further 1 minute, stirring and shaking the wok continuously. Stir in the sugar, soy sauce, chicken stock, salt and pepper. Simmer until all the ingredients are blended. Serve piping hot.

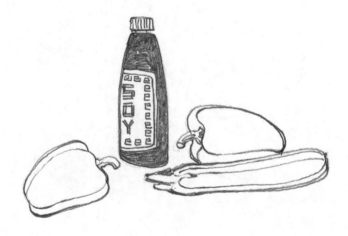

STUFFED MANGETOUT

Stuffed mangetout are impressive as people cannot fail to notice that they are quite fiddley to prepare! Chopped mussels or prawns could be used in place of the abalone.

Serves 4

INGREDIENTS
12 large mangetout, trimmed
1 tbsp oil
½ tsp chopped fresh root ginger
1 spring onion, chopped
4 pieces abalone, diced
1 tbsp soy sauce
Salt and freshly ground black
    pepper

For the Sauce
1 tbsp vinegar
1 tsp sugar
1 tbsp soy sauce
1 tbsp freshly chopped herbs

Blanch the mangetout in boiling, lightly salted water for 1-2 minutes, then set aside to drain. Slit the mangetout along one side of the pods, remove the small peas from inside and reserve.

Heat the oil in a wok and stir-fry the ginger, spring onion, abalone and the small peas for 3 minutes. Stir in the soy sauce and continue cooking until the soy sauce has evaporated. Season with salt and pepper. Fill each of the mangetout with the stuffing and place them side by side in a Chinese steamer. Steam until completely heated through, about 4-5 minutes. Mix together the sauce ingredients and serve the sauce with the hot stuffed mangetout.

STEAMED COURGETTE FLOWERS

If you grow your own courgettes and can harvest your own courgette flowers you may like to try this recipe. It is virtually impossible, unless you are a top chef, to buy courgette flowers.

Serves 4

INGREDIENTS

460g/1lb boned shoulder of pork
½ onion
1 tbsp oil
½ tsp chopped fresh root ginger
2 tbsps soy sauce
12 small courgettes with their
flowers attached
1 drop vinegar
2 tsps sesame oil
Salt and freshly ground black
pepper

Cut the pork shoulder and the onion into very small cubes. Heat the oil in a wok and stir-fry the ginger, pork and onion for 1 minute. Stir in ½ tsp of soy sauce and set aside.

Wash the courgettes and their flowers, then steam them for 30 seconds in a Chinese steamer. Refresh them by plunging into cold water. Open up the flowers, by stretching them gently with your fingers. Stuff the meat filling inside the flowers, down between the petals. Close the flowers again by pulling the petals back into place, forming a ball at the end of each courgette. Put the courgettes back in the steamer and cook for 4 minutes. Reheat the remaining meat stuffing in the wok. Mix together the remaining soy sauce, the vinegar and sesame oil and season with salt and pepper. Pour this sauce over the courgettes and their flowers. Serve with the reheated filling.

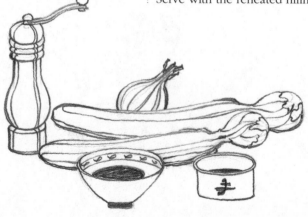

SPECIAL MIXED VEGETABLES

The secret of success with any stir-fry is to have all the ingredients prepared and chopped before you heat the wok. With such a quick cooking time this is very important.

Serves 4

INGREDIENTS

3 tomatoes, skinned, seeded and quartered
1 tbsp oil
1 clove garlic, crushed
2.5cm/1 inch piece fresh root ginger, peeled and sliced
4 Chinese leaves, shredded
60g/2oz flat mushrooms, thinly sliced
60g/2oz bamboo shoots, sliced
3 sticks celery, sliced diagonally
60g/2oz baby corn, cut in half if large
1 small red pepper, seeded and thinly sliced
60g/2oz bean sprouts
2 tbsps light soy sauce
Dash of sesame oil
Salt and freshly ground black pepper

Skin the tomatoes by plunging them into boiling water for 5 seconds. Remove them with a slotted spoon and place in a bowl of cold water. This will make the skins easier to remove. Slip off the skins. Cut out the core using a small sharp knife. Cut the tomatoes in half and then in quarters. Use a teaspoon or a serrated edged knife to remove the seeds. Reserve the tomatoes – they are added to the wok last.

Heat the oil in a wok and add the ingredients in the order given, up to and including the beansprouts. Stir-fry the vegetables for about 2 minutes. Stir in the soy sauce and sesame oil and add the tomatoes. Heat through for 30 seconds then serve immediately.

STIR-FRIED TARO AND CARROTS

Taro is a relative of the yam and is very much like the eddo, which is available in many supermarkets. Eddo, which is slightly smaller than taro, may also be used for this recipe.

Serves 4

INGREDIENTS
460g/1lb taro
1 tbsp oil
225g/8oz carrots, peeled and cut
  into rounds
2 tsps hoisin sauce
120ml/4 fl oz beef stock
Salt and freshly ground black
  pepper

Peel the taro and cut it into thin slices, and then into matchsticks. Heat the oil in a wok and stir-fry the carrots and taro for 3 minutes, shaking the wok frequently. Add the hoisin sauce and the stock and continue to cook until slightly caramelised. Season with salt and pepper and serve hot. The vegetables should still be quite crisp.

BRAISED AUBERGINES

I love aubergines cooked in any way, in any dish. Served braised, the real flavour of this delicious vegetable is allowed to develop and delight.

Serves 6, or 3 as a main dish

INGREDIENTS
3 medium aubergines
150ml/¼ pint stock
2 tbsps soy sauce
½ tsp sugar
2 tbsps pale dry sherry
2 tbsps finely chopped spring
  onions

Preheat the oven to 190°C/375°F/Gas Mark 5. Cut the aubergines in half lengthways and lay, cut side down, in a large flat casserole dish. Mix the stock with the soy sauce, sugar and sherry and pour over the aubergines. Cover with a lid or foil and cook in the preheated oven for 1 hour. Baste the aubergines once during cooking. Serve garnished with the finely chopped spring onions.

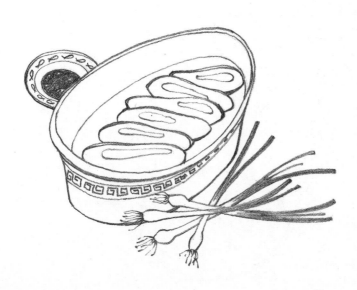

SESAME STIR-FRY

The sesame seeds give an unusual crunch to this vegetable stir-fry. Served with egg fried rice it would make an excellent supper dish for 2 people.

Serves 4

INGREDIENTS

2 tbsps vegetable oil
½ tsp grated fresh root ginger
15g/½oz sesame seeds
60g/2oz mangetout
1 stick celery, sliced
2 baby sweetcorns, cut in half
  lengthways
60g/2oz water chestnuts, thinly
  sliced
30g/1oz mushrooms, thinly sliced
2 spring onions, sliced diagonally
½ red pepper, seeded and sliced
120g/4oz Chinese leaves, washed
  and shredded
120g/4oz bean sprouts
1 tbsp cornflour
2 tbsps light soy sauce
1 tbsp sherry
1 tsp sesame oil
4 tbsps water

Heat the oil in a wok or large frying pan and fry the ginger and sesame seeds for 1 minute. Add the mangetout, celery, baby corns, water chestnuts, mushrooms, onion and pepper, and stir-fry for 5 minutes or until the vegetables are beginning to soften slightly. Add the Chinese leaves and bean sprouts and toss over the heat for 1 to 2 minutes. Combine the remaining ingredients in a small bowl, then add them to the pan. Continue cooking until the sauce boils and thickens slightly. Serve immediately.

QUICK-FRIED SNOW PEAS WITH BEAN SPROUTS

Snow Peas is another name for mangetout and is much more romantic! This is a very simple dish to cook but the pickle and sesame oil flavour the vegetables well, making an unusual and exciting dish.

Serves 4

INGREDIENTS
340g/12oz snow peas or
  mangetout
1 tbsp Szechuan pickles
4 tbsps oil
460g/1lb bean sprouts
2 tsps salt
3 tbsps water
2 tsps sesame oil

Finely shred the mangetout and chop the pickle. Heat the oil in a large wok, add the mangetout and pickle and stir-fry for 2 minutes. Add the bean sprouts, salt and water and cook for a further 2 minutes. Sprinkle the vegetables with the sesame oil and serve immediately.

MU SHU ROU

'Golden needles' are the dried buds of a type of lilly, and wood ears are a variety of dried mushroom. They may be difficult to obtain if you do not have a Chinese supermarket close by, in which case use 8-10 ordinary Chinese dried mushrooms and omit the 'golden needles'.

Serves 4

INGREDIENTS

2 tbsps 'wood ears'
4 Chinese dried mushrooms
2 stalks 'golden needles'
225g/8oz minced pork
3 tsps soy sauce
2 tsps water
Salt and freshly ground black
  pepper
3 spring onions
2 slices fresh root ginger, peeled
3 eggs, lightly beaten
1 tsp salt
5 tbsps oil
1 tsp seasame oil
1 tsp pale dry sherry
Peking Pancakes (see recipe for
  Peking Duck) or lettuce to
  serve

Soak both types of dried mushrooms in hot water for 15 minutes. Soak the golden needles in hot water for 30 minutes then tie together, knotting in the centre to prevent them from falling apart during cooking. Drain and squeeze out excess water.

Mix the pork with the soy sauce, water, salt and pepper and leave for 10 minutes. Drain and shred the mushrooms, removing any tough stalks. Drain the liquid from the pork. Shred the spring onions and the root ginger, and beat the eggs in a small bowl with the salt.

Heat half the oil in a large frying pan or wok. Add the mushrooms, golden needles and ginger and stir-fry for 1 minute, then add the pork and cook for a further 2 minutes. Add the spring onions, stir-fry briefly and then remove all the contents of the wok with a slotted spoon.

Heat the remaining oil in the wok, then add the beaten eggs. Cook until just set, then return the pork and mushroom mixture to the wok, stirring to mix with the egg. Sprinkle with the sesame oil and sherry.

Serve hot, wrapped in pancakes or crisp lettuce leaves.

TEN VARIETIES OF BEAUTY

The title of this recipe refers to the ten vegetables in it. Ten Varieties of Beauty sounds much better than Ten Vegetable Stir-fry!

Serves 4

INGREDIENTS
10 dried Shiitake mushrooms
2 carrots
4 tbsps vegetable oil
3 sticks celery, trimmed and
　sliced diagonally
90g/3oz mangetout
8 baby corns, cut in half
　lengthways
1 red pepper, seeded and sliced
4 spring onions, sliced
60g/2oz bean sprouts
10 water chestnuts, sliced
60g/2oz sliced bamboo shoots,
　drained
280ml/½ pint vegetable stock
2 tbsps cornflour
3 tbsps light soy sauce
1 tsp sesame oil

Place the mushrooms in a bowl and add boiling water to cover. Leave to stand for 30 minutes, then drain and discard the stalks. Cut the carrots into ribbons using a potato peeler.

Heat the oil in a wok or large frying pan and fry the celery, mangetout and baby corns for 3 minutes. Add the red pepper and carrots and stir-fry for 2 minutes, then stir in the remaining vegetables and stir-fry for 3 to 4 minutes, or until the vegetables are cooked but still crisp. Add the stock to the pan. Combine the cornflour, soy sauce and sesame oil and stir into the pan. Cook, stirring constantly, until the sauce boils and thickens. Serve immediately.

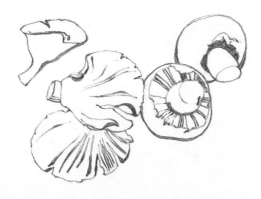

BRAISED CELERY WITH DRIED SHRIMPS & CHINESE MUSHROOM SAUCE

Braised celery is always a treat – with a Chinese Mushroom sauce and dried shrimps for extra flavour it becomes a most splendid dish.

Serves 4

INGREDIENTS

10 medium sized Chinese dried mushrooms
2 tbsps dried shrimps
680g/1½lbs celery
430ml/¾ pint chicken stock
1 tsp salt
1 tbsp soy sauce
½ tsp sugar
1 tsp sesame oil
2 tsp soya oil
1½ tsps cornflour
1 tbsp water
1 tbsp chopped spring onions

Soak the Chinese mushrooms in boiling water for at least 1 hour. Soak the dried shrimps in boiling water for 30 minutes. Preheat the oven to 190°C/375°F/Gas Mark 5.

Drain the mushrooms and discard the hard stems. Wash and trim the celery and cut into 10cm/4 inch lengths, then place in an ovenproof dish. Mix together 150ml/¼ pint of the stock and the salt. Drain the dried shrimps and add them to the stock then pour it over the celery. Cover with foil and bake in the preheated oven for 30 minutes.

Whilst the celery is cooking, place the mushrooms in a saucepan with the soy sauce, sugar, sesame oil, soya oil and the remaining 280ml/½ pint chicken stock. Bring to the boil then simmer for 30 minutes.

Mix the cornflour with the water and add any cooking liquor from the celery. Add the cornflour mixture to the mushrooms and bring to the boil, stirring all the time. Pour the thickened sauce over the celery and sprinkle with the chopped spring onions before serving.

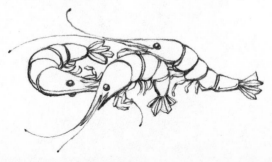

STIR-FRIED FRENCH BEANS WITH CHILLI

Hot and spicy green beans make an unusual and delicious Chinese-style vegetable dish.

Serves 4

INGREDIENTS
460g/1lb French beans
3 red chillies, seeded
1½ tbsps oil
1 tbsp light soy sauce
½ tsp sugar
½ tsp sesame oil

Wash and trim the beans then cut them in half. Cook in boiling salted water for 2 minutes, then drain and rinse the beans in cold water.

Shred the chillies finely after removing the seeds. Heat the oil in a wok and add the drained beans, chillies, soy sauce and sugar. Stir-fry for 3 minutes then add the sesame oil. Remove the wok from the heat and serve the beans immediately.

STEAMED CABBAGE ROLLS WITH FISH AND CRABMEAT

These stuffed cabbage leaves are mildly seasoned to allow the flavour of the fish filling to blossom. Serve with soy sauce and chilli sauce for dipping.

Serves 4

INGREDIENTS

8 large Chinese cabbage leaves
225g/8oz white fish fillets,
  skinned
2 slices fresh root ginger, peeled
1½ tsps salt
1 egg white
1 tsp sesame oil
225g/8oz crabmeat
Soy sauce
Chilli sauce

Pour boiling water over the cabbage leaves to soften them. Drain the leaves and dry well. Cut the fish into small pieces and finely chop the ginger. Place the fish and ginger in a bowl with the salt, egg white, sesame oil and crabmeat and mix well.

Lay the cabbage leaves out flat and divide the fish mixture between them, then roll the leaves up tightly. Secure the rolls with wooden cocktail sticks if necessary. Place the cabbage rolls in a small heatproof dish, then place the dish in a steamer. Steam vigorously for 10-12 minutes.

Serve the cabbage rolls with soy sauce and chilli sauce for dipping.

CANTONESE EGG FU YUNG

There are so many recipes for Egg Fu Yung cooked and enjoyed throughout China. Some use only egg whites but this easy recipe uses whole eggs and is served with a sauce.

Serves 2-3

INGREDIENTS

5 eggs
60g/2oz shredded cooked meat, poultry or fish
1 stick celery, finely shredded
4 Chinese dried mushrooms, soaked in boiling water for 5 minutes
60g/2oz bean sprouts
1 small onion, finely sliced
Salt and freshly ground black pepper
1 tsp dry sherry
Oil for frying

Sauce
1 tbsp cornflour dissolved in 3 tbsps cold water
280ml/½ pint chicken stock
1 tsp tomato ketchup
1 tbsp soy sauce
Dash of sesame oil

Beat the eggs lightly and add the shredded meat and celery. Squeeze all the liquid from the dried mushrooms, then discard the stems and cut the caps into thin slices. Add the mushrooms to the egg mixture with the bean sprouts and onion. Add a pinch of salt and pepper and the sherry and mix well.

Heat a wok or frying pan and pour in about 4 tbsps oil. When hot, carefully spoon in about 90ml/3 fl oz of the egg mixture. Cook until brown on one side, turn over gently and brown the other side. Remove the cooked egg to a plate and continue until all the mixture is cooked. Combine all the sauce ingredients in a small, heavy-based pan, season with salt and pepper and bring slowly to the boil, stirring continuously until thickened and cleared. Pour the sauce over the Egg Fu Yung to serve.

AUBERGINES & PEPPERS
SZECHUAN-STYLE

*This hot vegetable dish could be served on its own with rice,
or with a chicken or meat dish. Szechuan food is hot – you
may adjust the chillies to suit your own taste!*

Serves 4

INGREDIENTS

1 large aubergine
Oil for deep-frying
2 cloves garlic, crushed
2.5cm/1 inch piece fresh ginger,
    peeled and shredded
1 onion, cut into 2.5cm/1 inch
    pieces
1 small green pepper, seeded,
    and cut into 2.5cm/1 inch
    pieces
1 small red pepper, seeded and
    cut into 2.5cm/1 inch pieces
1 red or green chilli, seeded, and
    cut into thin strips
120ml/4 fl oz chicken or
    vegetable stock
1 tbsp sugar
1 tsp vinegar
Salt and freshly ground black
    pepper
1 tsp cornflour
1 tbsp soy sauce
Dash of sesame oil

Cut the aubergine in half and
score the cut surface with a
sharp knife. Sprinkle lightly with
salt and leave to drain in a
colander, or on absorbent
kitchen paper for 30 minutes.
Squeeze the aubergine gently to
extract any bitter juices, then
rinse thoroughly under cold
water. Pat dry then cut the
aubergine into 2.5cm/1 inch
cubes.

Heat about 3 tbsps oil in a wok.
Add the aubergine and stir-fry for
about 4-5 minutes. It may be
necessary to add more oil as the
aubergine cooks. Remove the
aubergine from the wok and set
aside.

Reheat the wok and add 2 tbsps
oil. Add the garlic and ginger and
stir-fry for 1 minute, then add the
onions and stir-fry for 2 minutes.
Add the green pepper, red
pepper and chilli and stir-fry for
1 minute. Return the aubergine
to the wok with the remaining
ingredients. Bring to the boil,
stirring constantly, and cook until
the sauce thickens and clears.
Serve immediately.

MUSHROOM STEW

*A variety of mushrooms, each with their own colour and
flavour, is the secret of this dish. Oyster sauce is a perfect
seasoning for mushrooms.*

Serves 4

INGREDIENTS
225g/8oz Chinese dried black
  mushrooms, soaked for 15
  minutes in warm water
225g/8oz Chinese dried
  mushrooms, any variety,
  soaked for 15 minutes in warm
  water
1 tbsp oil
2-3 cloves garlic, chopped
1 tbsp chopped fresh root ginger
280ml/½ pint chicken stock
1 tbsp oyster sauce
Salt and freshly ground black
  pepper

Cook the mushrooms in boiling,
lightly salted water for 45
minutes. Rinse under cold water
and set aside to drain. Heat the
oil in a wok and stir-fry the garlic
and ginger. Add the mushrooms
and cook briefly, then add the
stock, followed by the oyster
sauce and salt and pepper to
taste. Continue cooking until the
sauce is thick and coats the
mushrooms. Serve hot.

STIR-FRIED TOFU SALAD

Stir-fried vegetables do not have to be eaten hot and, once cooled, they make deliciously crunchy salads. By adding tofu you are adding stacks of protein, making a complete dish which requires no accompaniment.

Serves 4-6

INGREDIENTS

225g/8oz tofu or bean curd
120g/4oz mangetout
60g/2oz mushrooms
2 carrots
2 sticks celery
4 spring onions
150ml/¼ pint vegetable oil
60g/2oz broccoli florets
3 tbsps lemon juice
2 tsps honey
1 tsp grated fresh root ginger
3 tbsps soy sauce
Dash sesame oil
60g/2oz unsalted roasted peanuts
120g/4oz bean sprouts
½ head Chinese leaves

Drain the tofu well and press gently to remove any excess moisture. Cut into 1.25cm/½-inch cubes. Trim the tops and tails from the mangetout, and thinly slice the mushrooms. Slice the carrots and celery thinly, cutting at an angle to produce diagonal pieces, then trim the spring onions and slice them in the same way.

Heat 2 tbsps of the vegetable oil in a wok or large frying pan. Stir in the mangetout, mushrooms, celery, carrots and broccoli, and cook for 2 minutes, stirring constantly. Remove the vegetables from the wok with a slotted spoon and set them aside to cool. Place the remaining oil in a small bowl and whisk in the lemon juice, honey, ginger, soy sauce and sesame oil. Stir the sliced spring onions, peanuts and bean sprouts into the cooled vegetables, then mix the dressing into the vegetables, adding the tofu and tossing very carefully so that it does not break up while being mixed into the vegetables.

Shred the Chinese leaves and arrange them on a serving platter. Pile the salad ingredients over the top and serve the salad well chilled.

SPINACH & RADISH SALAD

*You could prepare this salad with small red radishes,
although daikon or mooli would be more traditional. Use
one daikon and half a bunch of red radishes for extra
colour.*

Serves 4-6

INGREDIENTS
1 bunch radishes
Salt and freshly ground black
  pepper
900g/2lbs young spinach leaves
2 tbsps light soy sauce
Pinch of sugar

Clean and trim the radishes and
slice them very finely, then
sprinkle lightly with salt. Wash
the spinach and remove any
woody stems. Place in a colander
and pour boiling water over the
spinach to blanch it. Shake
vigorously and dry on a clean
tea-towel.

Place the spinach in a salad bowl
and sprinkle with the soy sauce
and seasonings. Add the radish
and toss together before serving.

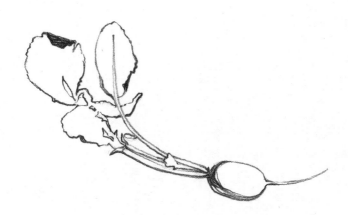

SPICED BEAN SPROUTS WITH CUCUMBER SHREDS

The savouriness of the dried shrimps makes this a crunchy salad with a difference.

Serves 6

INGREDIENTS
60g/2oz dried shrimps
900g/2lbs bean sprouts
½ cucumber

Sauce
1 tbsp soy sauce
1 tsp salt
1 tbsp vinegar
1½ tsps sesame oil
1 tsp sugar

Soak the dried shrimps in boiling water for 30 minutes. Wash the bean sprouts then place them in a colander and pour boiling water over them. Drain well, then drain the shrimps. Thinly shred the cucumber.

Mix all the ingredients for the sauce together. Arrange the cucumber on a platter or in the bottom of a salad bowl, place the bean sprouts on top, and then the dried shrimps. Pour the sauce over just before serving.

COLD TOSSED BEAN CURD

I always find tofu rather bland and tasteless but with this spicy sauce it is full of punchy flavour. Leave to marinade for at least 1 hour, for the tofu to become well seasoned.

Serves 4-6

INGREDIENTS
460g/1lb tofu or bean curd
2 tbsps chopped Szechuan
   pickles
2 tbsps dried shrimps, soaked in
   boiling water for 30 minutes
2 spring onions, chopped
3 tbsps oil
1 tbsp sesame oil
2 tbsps soy sauce
Salt
1 tbsp lemon juice
3 cloves garlic, chopped
½ tsp sugar
¼ tsp freshly ground black
   pepper

Dice the bean curd into small, bite-sized pieces, and place in a bowl. Sprinkle with the pickles, soaked and well drained shrimps and chopped spring onions.

Mix together all the remaining ingredients and pour them over the bean curd. Leave to marinade for at least 1 hour. Serve chilled.

CHINESE SALAD

Canned bamboo shoots and palm hearts may be used for this recipe if the fresh vegetables are not available - they will not be quite as crisp but add interesting flavours to the salad.

Serves 4

INGREDIENTS
1 head lettuce, washed and dried
4 slices ham, cut into thin strips
120g/4oz bamboo shoots
225g/8oz bean sprouts, blanched in boiling water and drained well
1 carrot, cut into thin strips
3 palm hearts, cut in half lengthways and then in half again
½ cucumber, cut into thin strips

Sauce
½ tsp vinegar
1 tbsp soy sauce
1 tbsp oil
1 tsp sugar
Salt and and freshly ground black pepper

Shred the lettuce leaves finely and mix them with the ham. Arrange on a serving plate. Prepare the bamboo shoots by slicing them first into long pieces, and then cutting the pieces in half. Blanch for 2 minutes and drain. Sprinkle the bean sprouts over the lettuce and place the bamboo shoots on top. Garnish the salad with the other vegetables, making the dish look as attractive as possible. Mix together the sauce ingredients and pour them over the prepared salad just before serving.

CHINESE LEAF SALAD WITH MUSHROOMS

This is a warm salad of Chinese leaves with a black mushroom sauce. Adding the sesame oil at the end of cooking really brings out all the flavours.

Serves 4

INGREDIENTS

12 Chinese dried black
   mushrooms, soaked for 15
   minutes in warm water
½ head Chinese leaves
1 tbsp peanut oil
½ clove garlic, chopped
1 tbsp sugar
2 tbsps soy sauce
1 tbsp freshly chopped parsley
Salt and freshly ground black
   pepper
Few drops sesame oil

Cook the mushrooms in boiling water for 15 minutes, then set them aside to drain. Prepare the Chinese leaves by separating the leaves and chopping each one into narrow strips. Blanch in boiling water for 1 minute, then refresh in cold water and leave to drain for 10 minutes.

Heat the oil in a wok and stir-fry the garlic, mushrooms and Chinese leaves for 2 minutes. Stir in the sugar, soy sauce and parsley and cook for a further 2 minutes. Season with salt and pepper, drizzle with the sesame oil and serve immediately.

BEAN SPROUT SALAD

Passata may sound very Italian to be an ingredient in a Classic Chinese recipe. They would traditionally use crushed tomatoes – passata is much more convenient.

Serves 4

INGREDIENTS
400g/14oz fresh bean sprouts
½ red pepper, seeded
1 carrot
½ cucumber
2 slices ham
1 large clove garlic, chopped
½ tsp chilli sauce
2 tbsps soy sauce
Salt and freshly ground black
    pepper
1 tbsp oil
½ tsp sugar
1 drop white wine vinegar
1 tbsp passata
2 tsps sesame oil

Cook the bean sprouts in boiling water for 5 minutes, then refresh them in cold water and set aside to drain and cool. Cut the pepper, carrot, cucumber and ham into thin strips. Mix together the chopped garlic, chilli sauce, soy sauce, salt and pepper, oil, sugar, vinegar and passata in a bowl to make a sauce. Toss together the bean sprouts, vegetables and ham. Pour the sauce and the sesame oil over the vegetables and serve chilled.

COLD TOSSED BEAN CURD
WITH DRIED SHRIMPS

*This spicy tofu salad should be served with raw mixed
vegetables or cold rice. Use any hot Oriental pickle if
Szechuan pickles are not available.*

Serves 4-6

INGREDIENTS
2 tbsps dried shrimps
2 tbsps white wine
460g/1lb tofu or bean curd
2 tbsps Szechuan pickles,
  chopped
2 tbsps chopped spring onions
3 tbsps oil
2 tbsps light soy sauce
1 tbsp sesame oil
1 tbsp lemon juice
2-3 cloves garlic, crushed

Soak the shrimps in the white
wine until softened, then drain
and chop them finely. Chop the
tofu into bite-sized pieces and
place in a bowl. Add the
shrimps, pickle and spring
onions, mix well and leave for 5
minutes. Blend the remaining
ingredients together and pour the
sauce over the tofu. Chill before
serving.

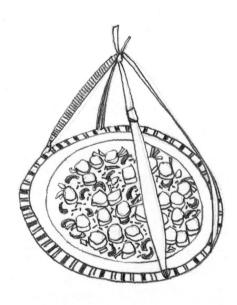

CHINESE LEAF AND CUCUMBER SALAD

This salad should definitely not be chilled before serving, otherwise the flavours will be retarded by the cold. I often think that salads are more flavoursome when served at room temperature.

Serves 4

INGREDIENTS
400g/14oz Chinese leaves, sliced thinly
1 clove garlic
1 tbsp soy sauce
1 tsp sugar
2 tbsps sesame oil
400g/14oz cucumber, sliced thinly
Salt and freshly ground black pepper

Blanch the Chinese leaves in boiling, salted water for 1 minute, then set aside to drain. Prepare the garlic by first slicing the clove in half and removing the core, then crush each half with the blade of a knife, and chop finely. Mix the garlic paste with the soy sauce, sugar and sesame oil. Mix the Chinese leaves and the cucumber in a serving bowl and season with a little salt and pepper. Pour the marinade over the vegetables and leave at room temperature for 2 hours. Toss and serve, still at room temperature.

RICE & NOODLES

It is easy to fall into the trap of thinking that rice must be served with all Chinese savoury dishes as, indeed, it often is! However, there are alternatives which include various types of noodles.

Rice – a Versatile Basic
Rice, or paddy fields, occupy almost 30 per cent of the total cultivated area of China and in the late 1980s the total annual production was around 172.4 million metric tons. It is therefore easy to see the importance of the crop to the country and to the cuisine.

Rice is eaten throughout China, although less in the north where it is actually too cold to grow the crop successfully. Noodles and dumplings are especially popular in this area as alternatives to rice – the dumplings are more satisfying in the colder climate.

Three Varieties of Rice

The Chinese use three varieties of rice, long-grain, short-grain and glutinous rice. Purists would not contemplate the use of 'easy-cook' varieties, stressing that it lacks both the colour and flavour of the long-grain rice grown in southern China. Short-grain rice is not what we in the west would call pudding rice, but a very slightly more rounded grain. It is used extensively for congee, which is traditionally served for breakfast. There are, however, many variations of congee which include meat or poultry and are served as part of a Chinese buffet, and there are also a few sweet congees.

Glutinous rice is the most unusual rice of the three. For years we in the west have been conditioned towards separate and fluffy grains, but this is a rice that cooks sticky – indeed, it is often called sticky rice! It is used for both sweet and savoury dishes, and is useful for stuffings. For the chopstick novice it is much easier to eat than separate grains! Glutinous rice has a high starch content which accounts for the way in which it cooks.

Boiled, 'Steamed' or Fried

Boiling is the most popular international cooking method for rice but the Chinese often steam it. This does not mean that it is cooked in a container over a pan of water, but rather that it is cooked very slowly in a measured amount of water, most of which is rapidly boiled away at the start of the cooking. As a rough guide, place your rice in a pan and add water to about 2.5cm/1 inch above the level of the rice. Bring to the boil, then cook quickly until all the water has evaporated from the surface of the rice. Reduce the heat to very low, then cover the pan with a tight-fitting lid and leave over the low heat for about 15 minutes, resisting the temptation to peep! You should then have perfect rice!

Fried rice is the most popular rice dish in Chinese restaurants in the west. It looks so interesting but, be warned! It sometimes has so many ingredients that it is more like a complete meal than an accompaniment to other dishes! There are several recipes for fried rice included in this chapter.

Chinese or Italian?

China and Italy both claim to have invented pasta and therefore noodles! Whoever made them first, both cuisines use them extensively. The Chinese use a variety of noodles although the most popular are soft, and made from wheat and egg, in the same way as Italian pasta. These may be boiled and served soft, or thoroughly dried to remove any moisture after boiling and then deep-fried to achieve crispy noodles which, I must confess, are my favourites!

Rice and Cellophane Noodles for Variety

Rice noodles are very popular in the rice growing areas of China, predominantly in the south, where they provide a welcome change from the more traditional method of cooking and serving rice. They are usually very fine and are most commonly used in soups. A thicker type known as rice sticks are flatter and thicker, more akin to pasta noodles, and may be used in a variety of recipes – they make an excellent dish akin to a special fried rice when mixed with prawns or shrimps, shredded chicken and crispy vegetables.

Cellophane noodles are not made from recycled packaging! They are actually made from a flour produced from ground mung beans and are most frequently added to savoury dishes as a filler, the complete dish then being served with rice. They are sometimes soaked to reconstitute them before being fried as a garnish.

FRIED RICE

This is a very basic recipe for egg fried rice, but one which can easily be adapted by adding cooked meat, shellfish, nuts, seeds or other vegetables. The secret is to get the rice and peas really well coated in the egg as it is just starting to set.

Serves 6-8

INGREDIENTS
3 tbsps oil
1 egg, beaten
1 tbsp soy sauce
460g/1lb cooked rice, well drained and dried
60g/2oz cooked peas
Salt and freshly ground black pepper
Dash sesame oil
2 spring onions, thinly sliced

Heat a wok and add the oil. Pour in the egg and soy sauce and cook until just beginning to set, then add the rice and peas and stir to coat with the egg mixture. Allow to cook for about 3 minutes, stirring continuously. Add seasonings and sesame oil. Spoon into a serving dish and sprinkle with the spring onions.

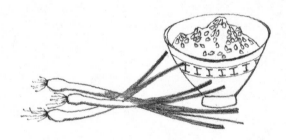

YANGCHOW SPECIAL FRIED RICE

There are so many different recipes for fried rice that I have become convinced that, for this versatile and savoury dish, anything goes! It is almost a case of adding whatever is to hand.

Yangchow Special Fried Rice is one stage richer and more elaborate than ordinary fried rice. It is prepared simply by adding 90-120g/3-4oz cooked pork and the same amount of shrimps to basic 'Fried Rice' (see recipe). It should not only be abounding with natural flavours, it should also be richly savoury because of the added pork and shrimps.

SHRIMP EGG RICE

With a simple salad garnish this shrimp egg rice makes an excellent lunch or supper dish. It is traditionally served as part of a Chinese buffet.

Serves 6

INGREDIENTS
460g/1lb long-grain rice
2 eggs, lightly beaten
½ tsp salt
4 tbsps oil
1 clove garlic, crushed
1 large onion, chopped
120g/4oz peeled shrimps
60g/2oz shelled peas
2 spring onions, chopped
2 tbsps dark soy sauce

Wash the rice thoroughly and place it in a saucepan. Add water to come 2.5cm/1 inch above the top of the rice. Bring the rice to the boil, stir once, then reduce the heat. Cover and simmer the rice for 5-7 minutes, or until the liquid has been absorbed. Rinse the rice in cold water and fluff up with a fork, to separate the grains.

Beat the eggs with a pinch of the salt. Heat 1 tablespoon of the oil in a wok and cook the onion until soft, but not brown. Pour in the egg and stir gently until the mixture is set. Remove the egg mixture and set it aside. Heat a further tablespoon of the oil and fry the garlic, shrimps, peas and spring onions quickly for 2 minutes. Remove from the wok and set aside. Heat the remaining oil in the wok and stir in the rice and remaining salt. Stir-fry, to heat the rice through, then add the egg and the shrimp mixtures and the soy sauce, stirring to blend thoroughly. Serve immediately.

STIR-FRIED RICE WITH PEPPERS

*This is a simple vegetable fried rice which goes well with any
number of stir-fried meat or fish dishes. The peppers make a
crunchy contrast to the rice.*

Serves 4

INGREDIENTS
120g/4oz long-grain rice
1 tbsp peanut oil
1 onion, chopped
1 green pepper, seeded and cut
  into small pieces
1 red pepper, seeded and cut
  into small pieces
1 tbsp soy sauce
Salt and freshly ground black
  pepper
1 tsp sesame oil

Cook the rice in boiling water,
then drain and set aside. Heat
the oil in a wok and stir-fry the
onion, then add the peppers and
fry until lightly browned. Add the
rice to the wok, stir in the soy
sauce and continue cooking until
the rice is heated through
completely. Season with salt and
pepper and the sesame oil and
serve.

SPECIAL FRIED RICE

Special Fried Rice is a meal in itself but it is usually served to accompany a variety of meat or fish dishes. I sometimes serve it with a selection of Chinese vegetables in season.

Serves 4

INGREDIENTS
2 tbsps peanut oil
2 eggs, beaten
Salt and freshly ground black
  pepper
2 spring onions, sliced diagonally
120g/4oz frozen peas
225g/8oz cooked rice
1 tbsp light soy sauce
1 tbsp dark soy sauce
120g/4oz bean sprouts
225g/8oz Chinese barbecued
  pork or cooked ham, diced
120g/4oz prawns or shrimps,
  shelled and de-veined
2 spring onion flowers (see
  recipe for Barbecued
  Spareribs) to garnish

Heat a wok and add 1 tbsp of the peanut oil, rolling it around the surface. Make a pancake by mixing the beaten eggs with a pinch of salt and 1 tsp of oil. Pour the egg mixture into the wok, and move the wok back and forth so that the mixture spreads over the surface. When the pancake is lightly browned on the underside, turn it over and cook on the other side. Remove the pancake and set aside to cool.

Heat the remaining oil in the wok. When hot, add the spring onions and peas and cook, covered, for 2 minutes. Remove the vegetables with a slotted spoon and set aside. Re-heat the oil and add the rice. Stir continuously over a low heat until the rice is heated through. Add both soy sauces and mix well, then stir in the peas, spring onions, bean sprouts, meat, prawns, and salt and pepper to taste. Mix thoroughly. Serve the rice hot, garnished with shredded pancake and spring onion flowers. The pancake may be sliced very finely and mixed into the rice, if preferred.

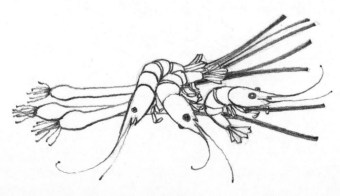

STIR-FRIED STICKY RICE

The Chinese favour a slightly rounded long-grain rice which cooks 'sticky' and is therefore much easier to eat with chopsticks than fluffy, separate grains.

Serves 4

INGREDIENTS
250g/9oz glutinous rice
2 tbsps oil
2 spring onions, chopped
½ onion, chopped
1 slice fresh root ginger, peeled
4 Chinese dried black mushrooms, soaked for 15 minutes in warm water, then drained and sliced
Salt and freshly ground black pepper

Wash the rice in plenty of cold water and place it in a sieve. Pour 1.14 litres/2 pints boiling water over the rice. Heat the oil in a wok and fry the spring onions, onion and ginger until golden brown. Add the mushrooms and continue cooking, stirring and shaking the wok frequently. Add the rice and stir well, then pour over enough water to cover the rice by 1.25cm/½ inch. Cover and cook over a moderate heat until there is almost no liquid left. Reduce the heat once again and continue cooking until all the liquid has been absorbed. This takes approximately 20 minutes in total. Add salt and pepper to taste and serve immediately.

DEEP-FRIED 'STICKY' RICE WITH PRAWNS

Long-grain rice processed to cook into separate, fluffy grains will not work for this dish! Use a shorter-grained rice – Thai rice is ideal – that will 'cook sticky' and is easy to shape into balls, if Chinese glutinous rice cannot be found.

Serves 4

INGREDIENTS

225g/8oz glutinous rice
20 large fresh prawns
1 tbsp oil
1 tsp finely chopped fresh root ginger
2-3 cloves garlic, chopped
1 small red pepper, seeded and finely chopped
1 small green pepper, seeded and finely chopped
1 onion, finely chopped
½ cucumber, finely chopped
1 tbsp soy sauce
Juice of 1 orange
2 tsps white wine vinegar
1 tsp sugar
120ml/4 fl oz chicken stock
Salt and freshly ground black pepper
Oil for deep-frying
1 tsp cornflour, combined with a little water

Steam the rice then allow it to dry at room temperature. Shell and de-vein the prawns. Heat the oil in a large frying pan or wok and briefly cook first the ginger and garlic and then the prawns. Remove with a slotted spoon and set aside. Stir-fry the red and green peppers, onion and cucumber until just cooked. Add the soy sauce, orange juice, vinegar, sugar, chicken stock and salt and pepper to taste, then return the prawns to the pan and cook over a low heat for approximately 10 minutes.

Meanwhile, heat the oil for deep-frying to 175°C/340°F. Shape the rice into balls and fry until golden. Drain on absorbent kitchen paper and place in a warm oven. Thicken the prawns and sauce with the cornflour, stirring until boiling, and serve the sauce poured over the rice balls.

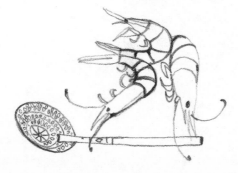

SINGAPORE FRIED NOODLES

These special fried noodles are a meal in themselves for 2 or 3 people, or may be served with Chinese vegetables in season.

Serves 2

INGREDIENTS
225g/8oz egg noodles
3 tbsps oil
2 eggs, lightly beaten
Salt and freshly ground black
  pepper
2 cloves garlic, crushed
1 tsp chilli powder
1 boneless chicken breast,
  skinned and cut into shreds
3 sticks celery, sliced diagonally
2 spring onions, sliced
1 red chilli, seeded and finely
  sliced
1 green chilli, seeded and finely
  sliced
225g/8oz prawns or shrimps,
  shelled and de-veined
120g/4oz bean sprouts
Chilli flowers (see recipe for
  Szechuan Fish) to garnish

Soak the noodles in boiling water for 8 minutes, or as directed on the packet. Drain on absorbent kitchen paper and leave to dry.

Heat a wok, and add 1 tbsp of oil. Add the lightly beaten eggs, and salt and pepper to taste. Stir gently and cook until set. Remove the egg from the wok and keep warm.

Add the remaining oil to the wok. When hot, add the garlic and chilli powder and fry for 30 seconds. Add the chicken, celery, spring onions and red and green chillies, and stir-fry for 8 minutes or until the chicken has cooked through. Finally, add the noodles, prawns and bean sprouts, and toss until well mixed and heated through. Serve with the scrambled egg, broken up with a fork and scattered over the top of the noodles, and garnish with chilli flowers.

CRISPY NOODLES

*When I was a child we sometimes used to have 'Vesta'
Chinese meals for a treat on Saturdays, and my favourite
part was always the crispy noodles! Now I know how to make
them myself there's no stopping me!*

Serves 4 with any stir-fry

INGREDIENTS
460g/1lb egg noodles
Oil for deep-frying
Salt
Sesame oil

Cook the noodles in plenty of boiling salted water for 12-14 minutes, stirring occasionally. Drain well, and pat dry with absorbent kitchen paper.

Fry the noodles in hot oil for 2-3 minutes until very crisp. Drain well. Sprinkle with salt and sesame oil, then serve immediately.

SOUTH SEA NOODLES

*I often choose to eat noodles instead of rice with a Chinese
meal. These noodles are almost a meal in themselves but also
go well with plainer meat or vegetable dishes.*

Serves 4

INGREDIENTS
2 tbsps Chinese dried shrimps,
  soaked
225g/8oz Chinese rice flour
  vermicelli or fine noodles
4 tbsps oil
2 medium onions, sliced
4 rashers bacon
2 tbsps curry powder
Salt
150ml/¼ pint chicken stock

Garnish
2 tbsps oil
225g/8oz shelled prawns
2 gloves garlic, chopped
4 spring onions, chopped
1 tbsp soy sauce
1 tbsp Hoisin sauce
1 tbsp pale dry sherry
2 tbsps freshly chopped parsley

Soak the shrimps in boiling water
for 30 minutes, then drain and
chop them. Cook the rice
vermicelli in boiling water for 3
minutes, then drain and rinse in
cold water.

Heat the oil in a wok, add the
onion, bacon and dried shrimps
and stir-fry for 1 minute. Add the
curry powder and a pinch of salt
and cook for a further 1 minute,
then add the stock and rice
vermicelli. Toss well to mix and
continue cooking for 2-3
minutes, then transfer the
mixture to a heated serving dish.

To prepare the garnish, heat the
oil in the wok, add the prawns
and garlic and stir-fry over a high
heat for 1 minute. Add all the
remaining ingredients and pour
the sauce over the noodles,
sprinkling them with the
chopped parsley.

PAOTZU STEAMED BUNS WITH PORK, CABBAGE AND MUSHROOMS

These are very light, filled dumplings, the yeast raising the dough and preventing the dumplings from becoming stodgy. Add extra flour during kneading if the dough is sticky.

Serves 4

INGREDIENTS
340g/12oz self-raising flour
30g/1oz fresh yeast
225ml/8 fl oz warm water
460g/1lb cabbage
6 Chinese dried black
   mushrooms, pre-soaked
2 slices fresh root ginger, peeled
225g/8oz minced pork
1 tbsp salt
1 tbsp soy sauce
1 tsp freshly ground black
   pepper
1 tsp sesame oil

Place the flour in a large bowl. Crumble the yeast into the warm water, stir and leave for 10 minutes or until frothy. Add the yeast liquid to the flour and mix well. Cover and leave in a warm place until doubled in size.

Chop the cabbage, mushrooms and root ginger finely, then place in a bowl and mix with the pork, salt, soy sauce, pepper and sesame oil.

Turn the dough out onto a floured surface and knead until smooth. Divide into pieces 4cm/1½ inches in diameter and press a little of the pork filling into each piece, shaping the dough around the filling into round 'buns'. Leave for 15-20 minutes. Place the filled buns in the top of a steamer and steam vigorously for 10-12 minutes. Serve immediately.

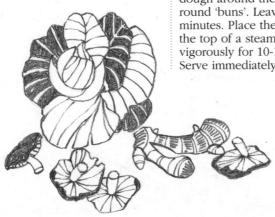

POT STICKER DUMPLINGS

*This descriptively named dish is so called because the
dumplings are fried in very little oil. To prevent them from
'pot sticking', ensure that they are well browned and crisp on
the bottom before they are steamed.*

Serves 4-6

INGREDIENTS
Oil for frying

Dumpling Pastry
175g/6oz plain flour
½ tsp salt
3 tbsps oil
Boiling water

Filling
120g/4oz finely minced pork or
  chicken
4 water chestnuts, finely
  chopped
3 spring onions, finely chopped
½ tsp five-spice powder
1 tbsp light soy sauce
1 tsp sugar
1 tsp sesame oil

Sift the flour and salt for the
dumpling pastry into a large
bowl and make a well in the
centre. Pour in the oil and add
enough boiling water to make a
pliable dough. Add about 4 tbsps
water at first and begin stirring
with a wooden spoon to
gradually incorporate the flour.

Add more water as necessary.
Knead the dough for about 5
minutes and allow to rest for 30
minutes. Divide the dough into
12 pieces and roll each piece out
into a circle about 15cm/6 inches
in diameter.

Mix all the filling ingredients
together and place a mound of
filling on half of each circle. Fold
over the top and press the edges
together firmly. Roll the joined
edges over using a twisting
motion and press down to seal.
Pour about 3mm/⅛ inch of oil
into a large frying pan, preferably
cast iron. When the oil is hot,
add the dumplings, flat side
down, and cook until well
browned.

When the underside is brown,
add about 90ml/3 fl oz water to
the pan and cover it tightly.
Continue cooking gently for
about 5 minutes, or until the top
surface of the steamed
dumplings appears cooked.
Serve immediately.

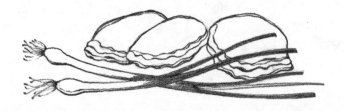

PEKING ONION PANCAKE

Peking Onion Pancakes are really more like a flour tortilla. They are re-rolled after filling to spread the onion evenly through the pancake. Serve with stir-fried vegetables.

Serves 4

INGREDIENTS
340g/12oz plain flour
225ml/8 fl oz boiling water
90ml/3 fl oz cold water
1 large onion, finely chopped
3 tsps salt
5 tbsps oil

Place the flour in a bowl and gradually add the boiling water, stirring continuously. Leave for 3 minutes then stir in the cold water and bring the mixture together into a manageable dough. Turn on to a lightly floured surface and knead well. Cover the dough and leave to rest for 20 minutes.

Divide the dough into 6 pieces and roll each into a 25cm/10 inch circle. Sprinkle them with chopped onion and salt, then roll up tightly and twist each pancake into a coil. Press flat with your hand, then roll out until each pancake is 6mm/¼ inch thick.

Heat the oil in a large frying pan and fry the pancakes for 3 minutes on each side. Keep warm while cooking the remaining pancakes and serve, cut into wedges.

DESSERTS

Desserts are a most unusual concept in the vast majority of Chinese households! There are very few truly classic Chinese dessert recipes and those that do exist have their origins in the Imperial Household, where the time and skills were available to experiment with food. The desserts that I have selected for this chapter show the limited variety of ingredients that are available for sweet dishes. I think that this contributes to the lack of enthusiasm with which Chinese desserts are greeted in the west - they are certainly not as highly regarded as the Chinese savoury dishes. Many desserts are really sweet dim sum, and are still widely served in teahouses.

Most Chinese families would be content to have a piece of fresh fruit to finish a family meal. There are many exotic fruits which, when freshly picked and at the height of their ripeness, would seem to be treasure enough to our western palates and it is difficult to imagine wanting anything else to conclude a meal. In China a selection of fresh fruits are sometimes served on a bed of ice to keep them very fresh. These are then dipped into sugar before being eaten, making a very simple dessert just a little more special.

Glazed Fruits – a Popular Tradition

One of the desserts which appears most frequently on Chinese restaurants menus (that is, apart from canned lychees and ice cream!) is apple or banana in a crisp sugar coating – the recipe for Sesame Toffee Apples is a delicious variation of this popular dessert. I personally feel that to call this dessert toffee apples confuses it somewhat with the apples that children in the west eat on sticks, but it is the same sort of idea! Sprinkling the fruits with sesame seeds after cooking gives a splendid texture and crunch.

Almonds – a Classic Ingredient in China

There are two types of almonds, sweet and bitter. Both are used in Chinese cookery, either as nuts or as essence or extract and many recipes do call for bitter almond essence. The bitter almonds and bitter almond essence are difficult to obtain in the west and you may have to be content with the regular almonds and their essence, although the resulting flavour of your dessert will not be strictly correct. I have always loved steamed or baked egg custards and sometimes add almond essence to make an alternative flavouring – you could try it with the recipe for Steamed Custard.

Almond tea should not be confused with tea as we drink it or even with green China teas. It is an infusion of ground nuts and rice boiled with water until almost a soup, and is best drunk cold. It can also be made into a more traditional dessert by setting it with gelatine or agar-agar, the vegetarian alternative. This is referred to as almond junket, but is not a junket in the true sense of a milk pudding set with rennet.

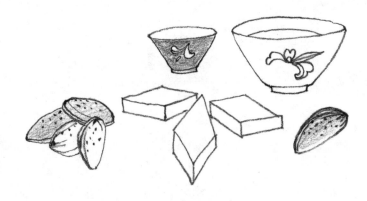

A Treasure Amongst Puddings

Perhaps the best known of all traditional Chinese desserts is, not surprisingly, a rice pudding! It is the Eight Treasure or Eight Jewel Rice, a moulded pudding set in a tin or a pudding basin and coated with a sweet syrup or liqueur before serving; the liqueur, if used, might be heated and flamed. A variety of glacé fruits and nuts are used and sweet bean paste or chestnut purée is spread in layers between the rice as the pudding is built up. This dessert is common at banquets and parties in China.

Sweet Wontons – the Perfect Solution

Although desserts are a treat in China there is a growing addiction to sweet nibbles or dim sum, which may be served almost like a chocolate or a petit four at the end of a meal. These are more common in restaurants than in the home as they are quite demanding in terms of both time and effort to prepare, but they do conclude a meal in a most satisfactory manner. Wontons, however, are a type of dim sum which may easily be prepared at home, using commercially prepared wonton wrappers. Once the folding technique has been mastered, to keep the filling safely enclosed during cooking, the preparation of the wontons is comparatively straightforward. Our recipe is for wontons filled with sweet bean paste, but small fruits or a thick purée of dates, for example, would also work well. These wontons are fried, drained and then lightly coated with a fragrant clear, runny honey before serving.

STIR-FRIED FRUIT SALAD

If you are unable to get all the fruits specified here, use a selection of exotic fruits from the supermarket.

Serves 4-6

INGREDIENTS
4 slices fresh pineapple
2 Asian pears
1 paw paw
1 grapefruit
6 kumquats
½ mango
12 lychees
2 tbsps oil
2 tbsps sugar
Ground cinnamon

Peel and core or deseed the pineapple, Asian pears and paw paw. Cut each into thin slices. Peel the grapefruit and cut into segments. Cut the kumquats into quarters lengthways or slice crossways. Remove the pips if wished. Peel the mango, and cut in half either side of the large central stone. Cut the flesh into thin slices. Peel the lychees.

Heat the oil and stir-fry the fruit in the following order: pineapple, lychees, kumquats, mango, Asian pears, paw paw and lastly the grapefruit. Sprinkle with the sugar. Cook for a few more minutes then sprinkle with the cinnamon. Serve hot or cold.

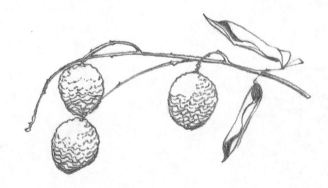

RICE PUDDINGS WITH CRYSTALLISED FRUIT

These puddings are very sweet and have an unusual, Oriental flavour. Use ordinary almond essence if bitter essence is not available.

Serves 4

INGREDIENTS
275g/10oz glutinous rice
4 tbsps sugar
90g/3oz crystallised fruit, chopped
2 drops bitter almond essence
20 dates, stoned
1 tsp oil, warmed

Rinse the rice first in cold then in hot water. Place in a saucepan and cover with water to a height of 1.25 cm/½ inch above the top of the rice, bring to the boil and cook, coverd, stirring occasionally. Once the rice is almost cooked, remove the pan from the heat – the rice will finish cooking in the hot water.

Stir in the sugar, crystallised fruit and almond essence. Set aside to cool.

Place the dates in a food processor and blend to a smooth, solid paste. Using your fingers, work the paste into 4 flat, even circles to fit 4 greased individual moulds or ramekins. (Use the warmed oil for greasing the ramekins.) Place a layer of rice in the bottom of the ramekins, top with a date circle and finish with another layer of rice. Cover the ramekins and cook in a steamer for 30 minutes, to allow the flavours to mix and develop. Allow to cool and then chill in the refrigerator before serving.

BANANAS COOKED IN COCONUT MILK

Many Chinese desserts are very sweet. This is lighter and less sweet than most, although a fair amount of sweetness does come from the bananas.

Serves 4

INGREDIENTS
1 tbsp brown sugar
120g/4oz desiccated coconut
430ml/¾ pint milk
4-6 large, ripe bananas, peeled and sliced diagonally into 3 or 4 pieces
Desiccated coconut, to garnish

Place the sugar, coconut and milk in a wok, and bring to simmering point. Remove from the heat and allow to cool for 15 minutes, then press the mixture through a sieve or a piece of muslin to squeeze out the juice.

Return the liquid to the wok, and simmer for 10 minutes, or until creamy. Add the prepared bananas, and cook slowly until they are soft. Serve immediately, sprinkled with desiccated coconut.

STEAMED CUSTARD

Egg custard is always a treat, and the traditional Chinese method of cooking it, by steaming, produces very light results.

Serves 4

INGREDIENTS
430ml/¾ pint milk
30g/1oz sugar
2 eggs, beaten
3 drops vanilla essence
Ground nutmeg or cinnamon

Place the sugar and milk in a wok or large frying pan and heat gently until the milk reaches a slow simmer and the sugar has dissolved. Pour into a bowl and leave to cool for 5 minutes. Meanwhile, wash the wok and place the steaming rack inside, with 4-5 cm/1½-2 inches of hot water. Return the wok to the heat and bring the water to simmering point.

Pour the milk and sugar mixture over the beaten eggs, beat again, and add the vanilla essence. Strain the custard into a shallow heatproof serving dish and sprinkle lightly with nutmeg or cinnamon. Place on the rack and cover the dish with greaseproof paper to prevent condensation from dropping into the custard. Cover the wok and steam for 10-15 minutes. Insert the tip of a knife into the centre of the custard to test if it is cooked – the blade should come out clean when the custard is set and gelatinous. Cover and cool for 1 hour, then place in the refrigerator until required.

EXOTIC FRUIT SALAD

Always buy exotic fruits a few days before you need them, to allow them to ripen fully. If they are very hard, leave them in an airing cupboard to ripen.

Serves 4

INGREDIENTS
1 papaya
2 kiwi fruits
4 rambutan fruits
4 canned lychees, plus the juice from the can
1 pomegranate
3 blood oranges
3 drops bitter almond essence, or ordinary almond essence

Peel all the fresh fruit except the pomegranate and the oranges, removing pips or stones as necessary. Try to buy a fully ripe papaya for the salad. Cut it in half and, using a small spoon, remove all the pips and any stringy skin around them. Peel each half, but not too thickly as the flesh immediately below the skin is very good. Finally, cut the flesh into thin slices or other fancy shapes. Peel two of the oranges. Remove all the pith and cut the flesh into segments.

Squeeze the juice from the remaining orange and mix it with the canned lychee juice and add the almond essence. Cut the kiwi fruit into slices, rounds or small cubes and combine these with the prepared papaya, rambutans, lychees and oranges in a bowl. Prepare the pomegranate by scoring the skin into quarters with a sharp knife. Break the fruit open with your hands and, using a teaspoon, scrape out the seeds. Add to the fruit salad. Pour the almond flavoured juices over and leave the salad to marinate for a few hours in the refrigerator. Serve chilled.

KIWI & COCONUT DUO

The green and white of these fruits are cool and elegant to look at, and the combination of flavours is unusual and refreshing.

Serves 4

INGREDIENTS
4 kiwi fruit
1 fresh coconut
A little sugar (optional)

Remove the ends of the kiwis. Peel them lengthways with a small sharp knife, then slice them thinly.

Pierce the three 'eyes' of the coconut with a screwdriver. Drain out the milk and strain it through muslin. Using a hammer, tap the coconut all around, about a third of the way down the shell from the eyes, until the coconut breaks open. Break the coconut into pieces and cut the coconut flesh into very thin slices. Arrange the kiwi slices on a serving plate and surround them with the slices of coconut. Add a little sugar to the coconut milk, if wished, and pour the milk over the fruit. Serve chilled.

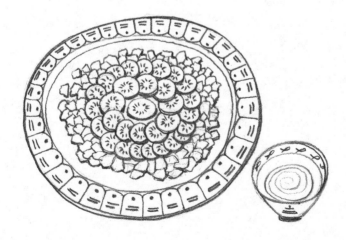

RICE IN MILK

Chinese Rice Pudding! Dare I suggest that you serve it with a dollop of jam in the middle?

Serves 4

INGREDIENTS
90g/3oz long-grain rice
570ml/1 pint milk
1 tbsp clear honey
¼ tsp ground cinnamon
5 cubes sugar

Blanch the rice in boiling water for 3-4 minutes, rinse well and set aside to drain. Pour the milk into a saucepan and stir in the honey, then sprinkle in the cinnamon. Stir in the well-drained rice and the sugar cubes. Cook over a gentle heat, stirring from time to time. Once the rice has absorbed all the liquid, remove it from the heat. Serve either hot or cold.

STUFFED LYCHEES

This might sound tricky, but it is very easy to pipe a filling into lychees, dates or any small fruit by using a forcing bag. A rigid forcing tube will not work so well.

Serves 4

INGREDIENTS
10 dates, pitted
2 bananas
Juice ½ lemon
20 canned lychees, reserving a
little syrup for the sauce

Place the pitted dates in a food processor and blend to a thick paste. Peel and mash the bananas with the lemon juice. Add the date paste and mix together well. Place the mixture in a piping bag and use to stuff the lychees. Mix the lychee syrup into the leftover stuffing to make a sauce. Serve the stuffed, chilled lychees with the sauce.

MELON SALAD

A honeydew melon could be used for this refreshing fruit salad, but I think that cantaloupes have far more flavour. Fruit salad is the perfect light pudding after a heavy meal of many courses.

Serves 4

INGREDIENTS
1 large canteloupe melon
1 mango
4 canned lychees
4 large or 8 small strawberries
Lychee syrup from the can

Peel and seed the melon and cut into thin slices. Peel and stone the mango and cut into thin slices. Using a melon baller, cut as many balls as possible out of the strawberries.

Arrange the melon slices on 4 small plates. Arrange a layer of mango over the melon. Place a lychee in the centre of each plate and arrange a few strawberry balls around the edges. Divide the lychee syrup evenly between the plates of fruit and chill them in the refrigerator before serving.

KUMQUATS WITH CRYSTALLISED GINGER

An Oriental variation on the classic international dessert of oranges in caramel. Kumquats are small tart oranges; a lime variety (limquats) is also available and is equally delicious.

Serves 4

INGREDIENTS
20 kumquats
2.5cm/1 inch piece fresh root ginger, peeled and sliced
225g/8oz sugar

Use a brush to scrub the kumquats. Blanch them in boiling water and drain, then blanch the root ginger slices and drain. Place the blanched kumquats in a saucepan with the sugar. Cover with water to a height of 5cm/2 inches above the fruit. Add the sliced ginger and bring to the boil. Reduce the heat and allow the liquid to reduce and caramelise gently. This is a long process, taking about 1½ hours. Add a little more water during cooking, if necessary. Allow the dish to cool after cooking and then chill in the refrigerator. Cut the ginger into very small pieces before serving.

ALMOND FLOAT WITH FRUIT

Sweet dishes or puddings are seldom served as part of a Chinese meal. There are, however, one or two really special desserts which are suitable for parties and banquets – this is certainly a party dessert.

Serves 6-8

INGREDIENTS
175ml/6 fl oz water
90g/3oz sugar
1 envelope powdered gelatine
280ml/½ pint milk
1 tsp almond essence
Few drops red or yellow food
   colouring (optional)
Fresh fruit such as kiwi, mango,
   pineapple, bananas, lychees,
   oranges or satsumas, peaches,
   berries, cherries, grapes or
   starfruit
Fresh mint for decoration

Sugar Syrup
90g/3oz sugar
570ml/1 pint water
½ tsp almond essence

Bring the water to the boil in a saucepan and stir in the sugar. Remove the pan from the heat. Sprinkle the gelatine over the water and leave for 1-2 minutes. Stir until the gelatine and sugar dissolves. Add the milk, flavouring and food colouring if used. Mix well and pour into a 20cm/8 inch square tin. Chill in the refrigerator until set.

To make the suagr syrup, mix the sugar and water together in a heavy-based pan. Cook over a gentle heat until the sugar dissolves, then bring to the boil and allow to boil for about 2 minutes, or until the syrup thickens slightly. Add the almond essence and allow to cool to room temperature. Chill in the refrigerator until ready to use. Prepare the fruit and place in attractive serving dish. Pour the chilled syrup over the fruit and mix well. Cut the set almond float into 2.5cm/1 inch diamond shapes or cubes. Use a spatula to remove them from the tin and stir them gently into the fruit mixture. Decorate with sprigs of fresh mint to serve.

EIGHT TREASURE RICE

The Chinese do not generally eat puddings except at banquets and special celebrations. This is one of the most famous puddings – use a pudding basin to cook and shape it in. Use brown dessert dates if jujubes are unavailable.

Serves 6-8

INGREDIENTS
280g/10oz pudding rice
60g/2oz lard
2 tbsps sugar
15 dried red dates (jujubes), pitted
30 raisins
10 walnut halves
10 glacé cherries
10 pieces of angelica, chopped
225g/8oz can sweetened chestnut purée

Syrup
3 tbsps sugar
280ml/½ pint cold water
1 tbsp cornflour blended with 2 tbsps water

Place the rice in a saucepan, cover with water and bring to the boil. Reduce the heat, cover with a lid and cook for 15 minutes or until the water is absorbed. Add the lard and the sugar to the cooked rice and mix well. Lightly oil a 1.14 litres/2 pint pudding basin and cover the bottom and sides with a thin layer of the rice mixture. Mix the fruits and nuts together and press into the rice. Spread a second, thicker, layer of rice over the first and fill the centre with the chestnut purée. Cover with the remaining rice and flatten the top. Cover with pleated greaseproof paper and foil and secure with string.

Steam the pudding for 1 hour. Just before it is cooked prepare the syrup. Dissolve the sugar in the water and bring to the boil. Add the cornflour paste and simmer gently until boiling, thickened and clear. Turn the pudding out onto a heated serving plate and pour the syrup over. Serve immediately, cut into wedge-shaped slices to reveal the layers.

SESAME TOFFEE APPLES

*This method may be used to caramelise many fruits but dry
fruits, such as apples and bananas, work best. The fruits
could be prepared up to the end of their second frying in
advance, and the wok cleaned ready for making the
caramel. The final stage of cooking is then quick and easy.*

Serves 4

INGREDIENTS
2 large, firm Granny Smith or
   Golden Delicious apples
1 tbsp flour
30g/1oz plain flour
30g/1oz cornflour
1 large egg, lightly beaten
1 tsp sesame oil
2 tbsps water
Oil for deep-frying
90ml/3 fl oz peanut oil
2 tsps sesame oil
9 tbsps sugar
2 tbsps white sesame seeds

Peel, core and cut the apples into
2.5cm/1 inch chunks, then toss
the apple pieces in 1 tbsp of
flour. Mix the 30g/1oz of flour
with the cornflour, egg and
sesame oil in a small bowl. Mix
to a batter with the water and
leave for 30 minutes.

Place the oil for deep-frying in a
wok, and heat to a moderate
temperature (180°C/350°F). Dip
the fruit in batter and coat well.

Deep fry several pieces at a time
until they are golden. Remove
from the oil with a slotted spoon
and drain on absorbent kitchen
paper. Continue cooking in
batches until all the fruit is fried.
Fry the fruit a second time in the
hot oil for 2-3 minutes, then
remove with a slotted spoon and
drain.

Carefully drain the fat into a
bowl to cool, and clean the wok.
Fill a bowl with cold water and
ice cubes, and put to one side.
Place the peanut and sesame oils
and the sugar in the wok, and
heat until the sugar melts. When
it begins to caramelise, stir and
add the sesame seeds and then
add all the fruit. Toss around
briefly and gently to coat in the
caramel. Take the apple pieces
out quickly, and drop them into
the iced water a few at a time, to
prevent them from sticking
together. Serve at once.

PEANUT BUTTER CAKE

Butter Cake is a popular Oriental dessert. Although light it is surprisingly filling, so only serve small portions.

Serves 4

INGREDIENTS

150g/5oz butter or margarine, softened to room temperature
90g/3oz sugar
4 eggs, separated and the whites stiffly whisked
120g/4oz plain flour, sieved
Pinch of salt
2 tbsps smooth peanut butter
1 tsp vanilla sugar, or ½ tsp vanilla essence + 1 tsp sugar
1 tsp grated lemon rind

Preheat the oven to 180°C/350°F/Gas Mark 4. Lightly grease a shallow 20cm/8 inch square baking tin. Beat or whisk the softened margarine and sugar together until light and fluffy. Add the egg yolks and beat them in well, then beat in the sieved flour and the salt. Add the peanut butter, vanilla sugar and the lemon rind. Beat well to combine all the ingredients. Whisk the egg whites in a clean bowl until they form soft peaks. Using a metal spoon or rubber spatula, gently fold in the egg whites, half at a time.

Pour the cake mixture into the baking tin and cook for 20-30 minutes, until the cake has risen slightly and is firm to the touch. Allow to cool before removing from the tin. Serve either slightly warm or chilled.

DATE DUMPLINGS

*I would serve these date dumplings with cream or custard
but a canned fruit in syrup, such as mangoes or lychees,
would also be good.*

Serves 4

INGREDIENTS
150ml/¼ pint water
150ml/¼ pint milk
2 tsps baking powder
1 tbsp sugar
Pinch of salt
400g/14oz plain flour, sieved
15 dates, pitted
1 tbsp ground almonds

Mix the water and the milk together then incorporate the baking powder, sugar and salt. Gradually stir in the flour and bring the mixture to a ball. You may find it easier to use your fingers rather than a spoon. Let the dough rest in a warm place for 1 hour.

Place the dates and the almonds in a food processor and blend until a smooth paste is formed. Roll out small lumps of the dough into circles on a lightly floured surface. Place a little of the date mixture in the centre of each circle then pull the edges up over the top, pinching them together well with your fingers to seal. Roll in your hands to form small balls. Steam the dumplings for approximately 20 minutes. You may need to do this in more than one batch. Serve hot or cold.

'HALF-MOON' BANANA PASTRIES

Bananas make a very sweet filling for these pastries. A sauce made with fresh oranges, a little sugar and a sprig or two of mint may not be traditional – but it's very good!

Serves 4

INGREDIENTS

Pastry
460g/1lb plain flour, sieved
120g/4oz lard
Pinch of salt
120ml/4 fl oz water

Filling
3 bananas
2 tsps sugar
Pinch cinnamon
Few drops lemon juice
1 egg yolk, beaten

Rub the lard into the flour with the salt. Using your fingers, incorporate the water gradually to form a ball. Wrap a damp cloth around the pastry and leave it to rest in a cool place for 30 minutes.

Preheat an oven to 180°C/350°F/Gas Mark 4. Peel the bananas and mash with a fork in a bowl. Add the sugar, cinnamon and lemon juice and mix well. Roll the pastry out thinly on a lightly floured surface, and cut into circles. Place a little of the banana filling on each round of pastry and fold into half-moon shapes, then seal the edges first by pinching together with your fingers and then by decorating with a fork. Continue until all the pastry and filling have been used.

Brush the beaten egg yolk over the half-moon pastries on a baking sheet. Pierce the pastry once to allow steam to escape during cooking. Bake for approximately 20 minutes, until crisp and golden.

SWEET BEAN WONTONS

Wonton wrappers may be stuffed with sweet or savoury fillings and are a typical teahouse, or café, snack. Sweet red bean paste is available in specialist Chinese food stores.

Serves 6

INGREDIENTS
15 wonton wrappers
225g/8oz sweet red bean paste
1 tbsp cornflour
4 tbsps cold water
Oil for deep-frying
Honey

Take a wonton wrapper in the palm of your hand and place a little of the red bean paste slightly above the centre. Mix together the cornflour and water and moisten the edge of the wrapper around the filling, then fold over, slightly off centre. Pull the sides together, using the cornflour and water paste to stick the two together, and turn inside out by gently pushing the filled centre. The wontons will be similar in shape to tortellini, the filled Italian pasta shapes.

Heat enough oil in a wok for deep-fat frying and, when hot, put in 4 of the filled wontons at a time. Cook until crisp and golden and remove with a slotted spoon, placing the wontons on absorbent kitchen paper to drain. Repeat with the remaining filled wontons. Served drizzled with honey.

ALMOND COOKIES

These almond cookies are very like western-style macaroons.
Allow them to cool slightly on the baking tray before
transferring them to a wire rack to cool completely.

Makes 30 cookies

INGREDIENTS
120g/4oz butter or margarine
60g/2oz caster sugar
30g/1oz light brown sugar
1 egg, beaten
Almond essence
120g/4oz plain flour
1 tsp baking powder
Pinch of salt
30g/1oz ground almonds,
   blanched or unblanched
30 whole blanched almonds
2 tbsps water

Preheat an oven to
180°C/350°F/Gas Mark 4. Cream
the butter or margarine together
with the two sugars until light
and fluffy. Divide the beaten egg
in half and add half to the sugar
mixture with a few drops of the
almond essence, then beat until
smooth. Reserve the remaining
egg for later use. Sift the flour,
baking powder and salt into the
egg mixture and add the ground
almonds. Mix well with your
hand. Shape the mixture into
small balls with your fingers and
place well apart on lightly
greased baking sheets. Flatten
the balls slightly and press an
almond on to the top of each
one. Mix the reserved egg with
the water and brush each cookie
before baking. Bake for 12-15
minutes; the cookies will be a
pale golden colour when done.
Cool on a wire rack.

INDEX